Curses and Boons in Indian Mythology

"pratibadhnāti hi śreyaḥ pūjya-pūjā-vyatikramaḥ"

(The neglect or violation of the reverence that is due to venerable persons obstructs well-being and prosperity.)

(Raghuvaṁśam, 1.79)

Curses and Boons in Indian Mythology

Dr. Sashikanta Barik
Laxman Majhi

BLACK EAGLE BOOKS
Dublin, USA | Bhubaneswar, India

Black Eagle Books
USA address:
7464 Wisdom Lane
Dublin, OH 43016

India address:
E/312, Trident Galaxy, Kalinga Nagar,
Bhubaneswar-751003, Odisha, India

E-mail: info@blackeaglebooks.org
Website: www.blackeaglebooks.org

First International Edition Published by
Black Eagle Books, 2025

CURSES AND BOONS IN INDIAN MYTHOLOGY
by **Dr. Sashikanta Barik | Laxman Majhi**

Cover & Interior Design: Ezy's Publication

ISBN- 978-1-64560-741-0 (Paperback)

Printed in the United States of America

Dedicated to Supreme Lord Shri Krishna

त्वदीयं वस्तु गोविन्द तुभ्यमेव समर्पये।

(O God, everything belongs to you and we are surrendering it back to you)

ॐ कृष्णाय वासुदेवाय हरये परमात्मने।
प्रणत: क्लेशनाशाय गोविंदाय नमो नम:।।

(Salutation to Krishna, Vasudeva, Hari the Paramatman, Govinda, we bow our heads to you for the destruction of all our grief.)

CONTENTS

Preface

The mythological heritage of India, preserved across millennia in its sacred texts and oral traditions, is a magnificent monumental artfact with intricate motifs of divinity, destiny, and human aspiration. In this vast canvas of myth, where gods and mortals weave their destinies amidst cosmic cycles, the twin forces of *śāpa* (curse) and *vara* (boon) stand as luminous threads, binding the ephemeral to the eternal. These potent acts of divine or human will ripple through the narratives of ancient texts, shaping the fates of heroes, sages, kings, and demons alike.

This book, "*Curses and Boons in Indian Mythology*", emerges from a keen scholarly desire to unravel the profound significance of these narrative devices and explore their roles as instruments of justice, transformation, and cosmic balance. Far from being mere supernatural pronouncements or miraculous endowments, *śāpa* and *vara* serve as critical catalysts within the mythic framework shaping destinies, altering cosmic order, and revealing the complex moral fabric of Indian philosophy. They reflect the eternal interplay of *dharma* (righteousness) and *adharma* (unrighteousness), embodying metaphysical principles of *karma*, *ṛta* (cosmic order), and divine will.

The purpose of this work is threefold: first, to document and analyze significant episodes of curses and boons from the primary mythic sources of India; second, to discern their symbolic and didactic functions within these narratives; and third, to contextualize these concepts within the broader canvas of Indian religious thought, emphasizing their enduring relevance in the contemporary cultural imagination. Through meticulous analysis and evocative storytelling, this book aims to guide readers into the heart of these narratives, offering insights into their spiritual, moral, and philosophical dimensions.

The scope of this volume extends across a wide spectrum of Indian mythological literature. It draws upon the *Vedas*, wherein the earliest intimations of divine blessings and retributive curses appear in hymnic invocations and cosmological myths; the *Itihāsa* the *Rāmāyaṇa* and *Mahābhārata* where *śāpa* and *vara* decisively influence the course of epic events; and the *Purāṇas*, those vast repositories of myth and theology, which elaborate upon these themes with profound moral insight. Beyond these classical sources, this work also explores regional myths, vernacular retellings, and oral traditions, revealing how the motifs of *śāpa* and *vara* have permeated diverse cultural landscapes, from the Tamil tales of Āṇṭāḷ to the Bengali legends of Manasā.

The importance of curses and boons in Indian mythology transcends mere narrative device. A *śāpa*, often born of righteous indignation or momentary lapse, serves as a moral corrective humbling the proud and restoring balance to a disrupted cosmic order. Conversely, a *vara* represents divine benevolence, a reward for devotion, penance, or valour, yet often fraught with unforeseen consequences. These acts are neither arbitrary nor whimsical; they are governed by the inexorable laws of *karma*, where every action reverberates through the universe, shaping the destiny of individuals and epochs alike. From the searing *śāpa* of a sage that humbles a monarch to a *vara* that grants immortality while binding its recipient in eternal suffering, these motifs underscore the delicate balance between free will and fate.

In crafting this study, an effort has been made to present these timeless narratives with a language both scholarly and poetic, inviting readers to immerse themselves in the beauty and complexity of Indian mythology. Each chapter unfolds like a lotus, revealing successive layers of meaning that connect the ancient to the contemporary, the divine to the human. Whether one approaches this work as a scholar of mythology, a seeker of spiritual wisdom, or simply a lover of stories, this book offers a journey through enchanted realms where every curse carries the seed of redemption, and every boon has the whispers of responsibility.

As you turn these pages, may you find yourself enthralled by the wisdom of the ancients, moved by the triumphs and tragedies of mythic heroes, and inspired to reflect upon the enduring truths that shape our own lives. Far in the interplay of *śāpa* and *vara*, we glimpse the eternal dance of creation, destruction, and renewal a cosmic rhythm that continues to resonate in the heart of India's mythic and philosophical heritage.

Bhūyāt sarva maṅgalaṁ

Introduction

In the luminous expanse of Indian mythology, where the divine and human intertwine, the concepts of *śāpa* (curse) and *vara* (boon) emerge as profound forces shaping destinies and illuminating the moral fabric of the cosmos. These twin phenomena, woven into the narratives of gods, sages, and mortals, are far more than mere literary devices; they are manifestations of the intricate interplay between free will, divine will, and the inexorable laws of *karma*. This chapter introduces their definition, philosophical underpinnings, moral significance, and unique role in Indian thought, while offering a comparative perspective with other ancient traditions.

Definition and Nature of *Śāpa* and *Vara*

A *śāpa* is a verbal pronouncement of misfortune, typically uttered by a spiritually empowered being either a sage (*ṛṣi*), a deity (*deva*), or enlightened mortal in response to transgression, disrespect, or a breach of *dharma*. Rooted in the Sanskrit verb *śap* (to curse or swear), a *śāpa* is not a mere expression of wrath but a potent act that alters the course of an individual's life, lineage, or cosmic sequence. Its power is derived from the spiritual authority and ascetic merit (*tapas-śakti*) of the one who utters it. Far from arbitrary, a *śāpa* operates within a moral framework that ensures eventual cosmic and ethical restoration.

Conversely, a *vara* is a supernatural gift or blessing bestowed by gods, sages, or spiritually accomplished beings in recognition of penance (*tapas*), devotion (*bhakti*), valour, or moral merit (*puṇya*). Derived from the root *vṛ* (to choose or grant), a *vara* may grant extraordinary abilities, immortality, divine protection, or even final liberation (*mokṣa*). Yet, many narratives caution that boons are double-edged, their misuse often invites downfall, as seen when Rāvaṇa's *vara* from Brahmā fails to protect him against mortal Rāma. Both *śāpa* and *vara* thus act as catalysts within mythic narratives, driving arcs of triumph, tragedy, and transformation.

Philosophical and Metaphysical Underpinnings

At their core, *śāpa* and *vara* are entwined with the metaphysical framework of Indian philosophy particularly the concepts of *dharma, karma, ṛta* (cosmic order), and *saṃsāra* (the cycle of rebirth). The Vedic worldview holds that the universe is sustained by *ṛta*, an eternal, unalterable moral order regulating both cosmic harmony and individual fate. Actions that uphold this order align with *dharma*, while those that disrupt it necessitate correction.

In this scheme, a *śāpa* acts as a corrective mechanism, realigning individuals with *dharma*. Its efficacy stems from the accumulated spiritual merit of the speaker, rather than divine caprice. Similarly, a *vara* is an articulation of cosmic grace, typically conferred in response to sustained *tapas* or unwavering *bhakti*, rewarding righteousness while cautioning against hubris.

A distinctive feature of Indian metaphysics is its belief in *vāk-śakti* (the power of the word). The *Ṛgveda* extols *vāk* as a creative force, capable of shaping reality itself. Curses and boons, spoken by spiritually potent beings, manifest as tangible, irreversible consequences. Nothing occurs outside the laws of *karma*, and both *śāpa* and *vara* function as instruments through which moral causality and cosmic justice are enacted.

Role in Moral Causality and Cosmic Justice

In Indian mythology, *śāpa* and *vara* serve as pivotal mechanisms of moral causality and cosmic justice, ensuring that every action resonates with inevitable consequences across lifetimes. A *śāpa*, while seemingly punitive, frequently operates within a larger teleological plan. It humbles the proud, corrects transgressions, and catalyzes spiritual growth. The *Mahābhārata*, for example, offers multiple instances of *śāpa*, such as Sage Durvāsā's curse on Śakuntalā or the Gandharva King, Chitraratha's curse on Karṇa each setting in motion transformative destinies.

Similarly, boons reward virtue and devotion, yet they test the recipient's wisdom and restraint. A *vara* may grant immortality or invincibility, but often brings unforeseen trials. The *Rāmāyaṇa* recounts how Rāvaṇa's boon of invulnerability emboldened his tyranny, ultimately inviting his fall through mortal hands illustrating that divine gifts carry responsibility.

Both *śāpa* and *vara* embody the principle that no deed, however minor, escapes consequence. They personify the philosophical idea that the universe is self-regulating through moral law, with sages, deities, and karmic forces acting as guardians of cosmic equilibrium.

Comparative Perspective with Other Ancient Traditions

The motifs of curses and blessings appear in various ancient civilizations, yet the Indian concept is uniquely nuanced. In Greek mythology, curses such as those of the Furies (Erinyes) or the generational curse of the House of Atreus mirror the Indian *śāpa* in their function as instruments of retribution. Yet, Greek curses often lack the redemptive possibilities integral to Indian narratives, where a *śāpa* may include conditions for release, reflecting the cyclical hope of *mokṣa*.

Greek boons (eukēsis), like those granted by Zeus or Apollo, parallel Indian *vara* in granting divine favour or miraculous powers, though typically devoid of the Indian emphasis on *tapas*, *vāk-śakti*, and karmic responsibility. Similarly, in Mesopotamian myths and Egyptian and Hebrew scriptures, divine pronouncements influence mortal fate but lack the complex interplay of *karma*, *saṃsāra*, and cosmic justice so central to Indian thought.

What distinguishes the Indian tradition is its deep-rooted belief in the metaphysical power of speech and asceticism, its emphasis on moral consequence extending across lifetimes, and its portrayal of both *śāpa* and *vara* as forces ultimately seeking the restoration of cosmic balance.

Conclusion

In essence, *śāpa* and *vara* are not isolated narrative flourishes but vital threads in the larger philosophical and cosmological fabric of Indian mythology. They articulate enduring truths about fate, moral causality, cosmic justice, and the human condition. Indian mythology vividly portrays the eternal dance of creation and destruction, justice and mercy, bondage and liberation a dance choreographed by the immutable laws of *karma* and *dharma*, where every word and action reverberates through the universe.

This introductory chapter thus lays the conceptual

groundwork for the exploration ahead, tracing the origins, functions, and philosophical implications of these powerful motifs through the sacred texts and oral traditions that constitute India's extraordinary mythological heritage.

❑

Chapter I

The Divine Dance of Boons and Curses

In the ethereal firmament of mythology, where gods and sages forecast destinies with whispers of divine will, the concepts of *vara* (boon) and *śāpa* (curse) stand as twin pillars of cosmic justice. These are not mere transactions of power but profound exchanges of energy, born from the depths of *tapas* (austere devotion) and *karuṇā* (compassion), or ignited by the fires of *krodha* (wrath) and *dharma* (righteousness). The *Purāṇas* brim with tales where ordinary mortals, touched by the grace of *divyātmās* (divine souls), ascend to extraordinary heights, while others, ensnared by their own misdeeds, plummet under the weight of celestial curses. This chapter explores the luminous boons that elevate and the shadowed curses that bind, revealing the intricate balance of sacrifice, sincerity, and cosmic consequence.

The Radiance of Boons: Gifts of Grace

Boons, those sacred bestowals of divine favour, are not mere whims of gods or sages but the fruit of arduous tapas and unyielding *sādhana* (spiritual practice). The *Purāṇas* recount how *devatās* (deities) and *ṛṣis* (sages), moved by the purity of a seeker's heart, grant *varas* that transform destinies. Consider the tale of Arjuna in the *Mahābhārata*, whose relentless penance in the forests of Indraprastha earned him the Pāśupatāstra, a weapon of divine might from Lord Śiva. Such boons are not won through fleeting gestures or hollow offerings but through a soul's unwavering commitment to *dharma* and sacrifice. As the *Bhagavad Gītā* (4.33) proclaims,

śreyān dravyamayād yajñāj jñānayajñaḥ parantapa /
sarvaṃ karmākhilaṃ pārtha jñāne parisamāpyate /

The offering of wisdom and devotion surpasses material gifts.

The beauty of a boon lies in its reciprocity. The recipient must embody *pātratā* (worthiness), a quality forged in the crucible of selflessness and sincerity. The *Upaniṣads* teach that the divine, though generous, is discerning. A sage like Viśvāmitra, who attained Brahmarṣi status through millennia of *tapas*, exemplifies this truth. His boon of spiritual ascendancy was not a gift lightly given but a recognition of his *sāttvika* (pure) resolve. Even in modern times, the blessings of mentors or the gratitude of those uplifted by acts of kindness carry the essence of *vara*, subtly shaping lives with prosperity and purpose.

The path to a boon is not paved with ease. The farmer toils under the sun, the artist pours their soul into creation, and the student burns the midnight oil each paying the price of effort to earn the earth's compassion or society's acclaim. As the *Taittirīya Upaniṣad* (1.11) advises, "*svādhyāyāt mā pramadaḥ*" never neglect your study and discipline. Without *tapas* (austere effort), the divine remains unmoved, for boons are not alms but rewards for those who align with the cosmic rhythm of *ṛta* (truth).

The Shadow of Curses: The Weight of Wrath

If boons are the light of divine favour, curses are the storm clouds of celestial retribution. A *śāpa* is not merely a punishment but a mirror reflecting the consequences of one's actions. The *Purāṇas* are replete with tales where the wrath of a *divyātmā* reshapes destinies. The sons of Sagara, reduced to ashes by Kapila Muni's curse, or King Parīkṣit, fated to die by a serpent's bite due to Śṛṅgi Ṛṣi's wrath, stand as stark reminders of the power of a sage's disapproval. Even in the *Rāmāyana*, Ahalyā's petrification by Gautama Ṛṣi underscores the peril of straying from *dharma*.

Curses, however, are not arbitrary. They spring from a violation of *dharma* be it deceit, betrayal, or harm to the innocent. The *Mahābhārata* narrates how Gāndhārī's anguished curse led to the Yadukula's annihilation, a consequence of their moral lapses. Similarly, the Yakṣa in Kālidāsa's *Meghadūta* suffers from separation due to neglecting his duties a poetic embodiment of karmic retribution. These stories illuminate a universal truth: a *śāpa* is a call to accountability, a force that compels the wrongdoer to reap what they have sown.

Intriguingly, curses extend beyond individuals to objects and places, as seen in modern anecdotes. The Hope Diamond, pilfered from a sacred idol, became a harbinger of misfortune, claiming lives and fortunes across continents. From the merchant Jean-Baptiste Tavernier to the ill-fated Evalyn Walsh McLean, its trail of tragedy underscores the notion that desecration invites cosmic reprisal. Similarly, a plot of land in Karachi, believed to house a saint's tomb, brought calamity to those who dared disturb its sanctity. These tales, whether rooted in myth or modernity, affirm that a *śāpa* is not mere superstition but a manifestation of disrupted harmony.

The Alchemy of Intent: Boons and Curses Intertwined

The interplay of boons and curses reveals a deeper truth: both are born from the same divine source, shaped by intent and action. A boon demands *tapas* and *pātratā*, while a curse demands accountability for *adharma*. The *Viṣṇu Purāṇa* narrates how Hiraṇyakaśipu's boon of near-invincibility, granted by Brahmā, became his undoing when his tyranny provoked Nṛsiṃha's wrath. Here, the boon and curse converge, illustrating that divine gifts are double-edged, their outcome shaped by the recipient's adherence to *dharma*.

The *Śrīmad Bhāgavatam* (7.5.19) warns, "*karmaṇā daiva-netreṇa*" actions are guided by divine will. A boon misused or a curse provoked by hubris serves as a reminder of the delicate balance between human endeavor and cosmic justice. The *Rāmāyana* teaches that Rāma's exile, though a seeming curse, became a boon through his righteous conduct, leading to his ultimate triumph. Thus, the divine dance of boons and curses is not a mere dichotomy but a continuum, where intent and action determine whether one soars to the heavens or falls to the abyss.

❑

Chapter II

The Subtle Mystery of Curses and Boons in Mythology

In the entire topography of Indian mythology, the concepts of *vara* (boon) and *śāpa* (curse) aren't just mere convenient plot devices; rather they are the basic artistic threads in myth narrative that determines the faith of characters. These twin pinary forces represent a profound metaphysical system, a cosmic scale where every act, thought, and intention is weighed. As we journey through the Purāṇas and ancient epics, we see mortal destinies rise and fall, not by accident, but as a direct result of these powerful pronouncements. This book explores the intricate mechanics behind these phenomena, delving into the principles of *pātratā* (worthiness), the immense spiritual energy of tapas (penance), and the immutable cosmic law of *ṛta* that governs them. We'll uncover how boons are not gifts to be demanded but blessings to be earned, and how curses are not acts of random vengeance but the fiery, inescapable consequence of a profound violation of *dharma*. Ultimately, the subtle mystery of curses and boons reveals a fundamental truth of the Indian worldview: that the universe is not chaotic, but a morally ordered cosmos where justice, both benevolent and retributive, is always served.

***Divya-śakti, Pātratā*, and the Cosmic Law**

In the iridescent glow of Indian mythology, the

phenomena of *vara* (boon) and *śāpa* (curse) operate not merely as narrative devices but as profound metaphysical principles governing the destinies of gods, sages, kings, and ordinary beings alike. The *Purāṇas*, those ageless chronicles of cosmic events, brim with narratives wherein mortal lives have been uplifted and transformed by the grace of a boon, or conversely, cast into misfortune by the sting of a curse. These are not arbitrary occurrences but outcomes dictated by the subtleties of merit (*pātratā*), intent, and the immutable laws of *ṛta* the cosmic order.

The Sanctity of Boons (*Varadāna*) and the Law of Deservedness

It is a well-acknowledged truth in the ancient Indian worldview that *divyātmā* enlightened souls bestow their grace only upon those who possess the requisite eligibility. As the aphorism goes:

"pātratāṁ vina dātuṁ na śakyate varaḥ"

(Without worthiness, a boon cannot be conferred.)

The *Purāṇas* recount countless episodes where kings, ascetics, householders, or even the downtrodden have attained impossible triumphs through divine favour, blessings born of inner purity, relentless *tapas* (penance), and moral steadfastness. However, these boons are never frivolously granted. Just as the earth yields grain only to the one who tills it, and the cow offers milk only when milked with care, so too do the divine forces respond to true effort, sacrifice, and virtue.

Not mere vocal pleas, gestures of flattery, or superficial offerings can elicit such gifts. Only profound inner emotion, marked by purity of intent and unyielding perseverance, can touch the heart of the divine. A *guru's* blessing, a mother's prayer, or a sage's glance when genuinely earned can uplift a soul from the abyss of despair to the zenith of fortune.

Boons: The Currency of *Tapas* and *Tyāga*

It must be understood that *tapas* are not the mere affliction of the body but a profound commitment to ideals, a readiness to sacrifice for the good, and the courage to endure hardship for higher principles. The *divyātmā* dispenses their *tapas-sampatti* the wealth of their spiritual merit only after discerning the recipient's worthiness, sincerity, and the potential consequences of their boon. An ancient adage asserts:

"dānād api varaḥ pradhānaḥ"

(A boon is nobler than a mere gift.)

While a material donation perishes, a boon alters fate itself, bringing a new dimension to destiny. Yet, even this sacred act is bound by ethical discernment. The *divyātmā* must contemplate: Who deserves this? For what purpose? What consequences shall arise?

The *Purāṇas* illustrate this principle through myriad narratives. Rāvaṇa, having pleased Lord Śaṅkara with austerities, received boons that made him nearly invincible, yet his unrestrained ambition brought his ruin. Conversely, *Bhakta* Śabarī's humble devotion earned her the grace of Śrī Rāma. Thus, while boons are potent, their bestowal is neither random nor indulgent.

Curses (*Śāpa*): The Fiery Fruit of Wrath

As welcome as the blessings of the wise are, equally terrifying is their wrath, manifesting as *śāpa*. When a person of immense *ātma-bala* (spiritual might) is deeply wronged, the consequence is not merely emotional, but cosmic. A *śāpa*, issued with righteous indignation, becomes an unalterable law of fate.

Ancient texts are replete with accounts where individuals, violating *dharma* or causing anguish to the virtuous, were consigned to dreadful fates. The *Purāṇas* remind us:

"aparādhān mahānṛṇāṁ śāpaḥ pātyati duṣkṛtam"

(The curse of the great falls heavily upon the wicked.)

The destruction of King Sagara's sons by Kapila Muni, the snakebite death of Parīkṣit due to Śṛṅgi's curse, and the annihilation of the Yadava clan as a result of Gāndhārī's grief-fuelled malediction are legendary illustrations of this principle.

Even material objects, lands, and relics have borne the imprint of curses. The ominous fate of the Hope Diamond and the tragic history of cursed artifacts across cultures reveal a consistent theme: when divine order is violated, repercussions ensue.

Curses in the Modern Context: The Continuance of Ancient Patterns

Even in contemporary times, such phenomena have not been relegated to mere myth. Stories of lands refusing habitation, artifacts bringing ruin, or individuals falling prey to inexplicable tragedies persist. The account of Tutankhamun's tomb, the misfortunes trailing the Hope Diamond, and cursed estates like those in Karachi reinforce the ancient belief that cosmic justice is inescapable.

While rationality dismisses these as coincidences or superstition, deeper inquiry often reveals patterns too precise to ignore. The law of causation (*kārya-kāraṇa-bhāva*) in Indian philosophy holds that every effect must have a cause, visible or subtle. Thus, curses, when viewed through this lens, are not irrational superstitions but metaphysical mechanisms to restore balance.

The Moral Foundation of Boons and Curses

Crucially, Indian wisdom maintains that neither boons nor curses arise unprovoked. A true *śāpa* emerges not from petulance but righteous indignation, and a *vara* flows not from indulgence but compassionate discernment. The case of Sage Durvāsā cursing Ambarīṣa, which rebounded upon himself due to the king's innocence, exemplifies that the misuse of such power leads to self-destruction.

This doctrine upholds a central tenet: *adharma* invariably attracts suffering, whether through natural consequences, societal retribution, or divine wrath. Those aligned with dharma need fear neither curse nor calamity.

"na dharmavān vinaśyati"

(The righteous never perish.)

Conclusion: The Enduring Law of Cosmic Equilibrium

The traditions of *vara* and *śāpa* are profound affirmations of the moral fabric underpinning existence. They emphasize that divine grace and righteous indignation are not arbitrary but deeply entwined with human conduct, intention, and merit.

As contemporary seekers, our task is not to dismiss these as relics of an archaic past, but to understand their symbolic, ethical, and metaphysical import. In the orchestration of cosmic law, these forces remind us that while fate may be mysterious, it is never unjust.

"*yad bhāvyam tad bhaviṣyati*" what is destined by the law of righteousness shall inevitably come to pass.

And within this eternal dance of cause and consequence, the phenomena of curses and boons continue to weave the intricate patterns of human destiny, in myth and in life.

❑

Chapter III

Curses and Boons in the Vedic Literature

In the ancient hymns of the Vedas, the earliest sacred texts of Indian civilization, the concepts of *śāpa* (curse) and *vara* (boon) emerge as primordial forces, woven into the very fabric of cosmic order and divine-human interaction. The *Ṛgveda* and *Atharvaveda*, in particular, offer profound insights into these pronouncements, revealing their roots in the spiritual authority of seers (*ṛṣis*), the metaphysical potency of the spoken word (*vāk*), and the ritual contexts that amplify their power. Though explicit narratives of curses and boons become more frequent in later *Itihāsa* and Purāṇic literature, the *Vedas* lay the essential philosophical and metaphysical groundwork for these transformative acts. This chapter explores their occurrences, functions, and underlying significance within Vedic literature, examining the roles of seers, gods, ritual speech, and mantra in sustaining moral and cosmic order.

Occurrences in *Ṛgveda* and *Atharvaveda*

The *Ṛgveda*, the most ancient and revered of the Vedic texts, primarily comprises hymns addressed to deities such as Agni, Indra, Varuṇa, and Soma. Though narrative accounts of curses and boons are rare, the philosophical notion that words carry both creative and destructive potential is deeply embedded. The hymns frequently invoke *vara* such as divine blessings in the form of longevity, progeny, cattle, rain, or victory in battle. For instance:

indraṃ vardhantu no giraḥ /

"May our words magnify Indra" (*Ṛgveda,* 1.9.1)

Such invocations reflect the belief that properly directed speech elicits divine favour. Conversely, the hymns also contain allusions to maledictions against enemies. While these are not always labeled as *śāpa*, the power of words to invoke misfortune or punishment upon wrongdoers is unmistakable, especially in relation to Varuṇa, the upholder of *ṛta* (cosmic order). In *Ṛgveda* 7.86, a poet pleads for release from Varuṇa's anger, suggesting the metaphorical noose (*pāśa*) as a binding curse that can be lifted through repentance and praise — a precursor to the redemptive potential of *śāpa* seen in later mythology.

The *Atharvaveda*, with its focus on practical rites, charms, and incantations, provides more explicit examples of *śāpa* and *vara*. Renowned for spells to curse enemies, ward off disease, and attract prosperity, it reflects a worldview where spoken words possess tangible, immediate power. For example:

yamasya pāśaṃ bibhṛtaṃ nuda te hṛdayād amīvām /

"May the noose of Yama be driven away from your heart" (*Atharvaveda*, 6.122.2)

Here, the mantra acts both apotropaically and as a blessing, illustrating the dual capacity of speech to harm and heal. Hymns like *Atharvaveda* 7.12 invoke prosperity and protection, functioning as *vara*-like pronouncements channeling divine energy for the benefit of the supplicant. In this way, the *Atharvaveda* bridges the abstract invocations of the *Ṛgveda* with the narrative-driven *śāpa* and *vara* of later epics and *Purāṇas*, grounding them in ritual practice.

Seers, Gods, and the Potency of Spoken Word

Central to the operation of *śāpa* and *vara* in the Vedic tradition is the sacred power of *vāk* (speech). The *Ṛgveda* (10.125) personifies Vāk as a divine goddess, the creative force through which the cosmos is shaped and sustained. This belief endows the utterances of seers (*ṛṣis*) and gods with extraordinary efficacy, making their words capable of altering destinies.

The *ṛṣis*, as *mantra-draṣṭāraḥ* (seers of sacred sounds), are not mere composers of hymns but visionaries whose speech, charged with *tapas* (spiritual energy) and divine insight (*dṛṣṭi*), functions as an instrument of cosmic justice. Their words, whether uttered as a curse or a blessing, manifest irreversible consequences within the cosmic order.

The deities too are approached as granters of boons and enforcers of moral consequence. Gods like Indra, Agni, and Varuṇa are frequently invoked in the Vedas to bestow health, offspring, prosperity, or protection. In *Ṛgveda* 5.3, Agni is extolled as a bestower of wealth and security, while Varuṇa in *Ṛgveda* 7.89 threatens punishment for transgression, aligning with the principle of *śāpa*. The authority of both seers and gods to pronounce curses or boons rests upon their alignment with *ṛta*, the cosmic principle ensuring that their words resonate with the eternal moral law.

The interplay between seers and gods reveals the collaborative nature of *śāpa* and *vara* in Vedic thought. A seer's curse often invokes divine sanction, while a god's boon is frequently mediated through a seer's hymnal praise or ritual offering. This synergy reflects a universe where human and divine agencies converge to uphold cosmic balance.

Ritual, *Mantra*, and the Pronouncement of *Śāpa* and *Vara*

The efficacy of *śāpa* and *vara* in Vedic literature is inseparable from the rituals and *mantras* framing their utterance. Vedic rituals, such as the soma sacrifice or *homa*, create a sacred environment where the human and divine realms intersect, amplifying the power of the spoken word. *Mantras*, chanted with precision and intent, are not mere words but vibrational forces that align with the cosmic rhythm of *ṛta*.

In the *Ṛgveda*, mantras function as vehicles for invoking *vara* for wealth, rain, progeny, or peace while certain incantations, more pronounced in the *Atharvaveda*, serve to curse adversaries or ward off malevolent influences. For example:

yad amīvām yad arāṭīm yac ca dūṣaṇam āśasaḥ /
tad āśīr atra dīrghāyuḥ kārṣītām indra sahaḥ //

"Whatever diseases, whatever evils and curses there are may mighty Indra drive them away." (*Atharvaveda,* 6.133)

Such *mantras* serve both protective and maledictory functions, illustrating how ritualized speech acts as a double-edged instrument of cosmic order.

The sacrificial priests (*hotṛ, adhvaryu, udgātṛ, brahman*) were believed to wield immense verbal power. A mispronounced *mantra* could provoke disaster, while a precise utterance could secure divine favour, wealth, and longevity. This belief in the infallibility of ritual speech prefigures the later *Itihāsa* and Purāṇic traditions where sages like Durvāsā or Vasiṣṭha curse kings and heroes, demonstrating the continuity of this concept throughout Indian sacred history.

Conclusion

The *Ṛgveda* and *Atharvaveda* offer the earliest glimpses of *śāpa* and *vara* as potent expressions of the spoken word's sacred power, deeply embedded in the metaphysical and ritualistic framework of early Indian thought. These texts establish the foundational belief in the creative and destructive potency of speech, revealing that both curses and boons were neither whimsical nor arbitrary but functioned within a moral and cosmic framework governed by *ṛta* and *karma*.

In positioning *śāpa* and *vara* as instruments of cosmic order and moral consequence, the *Vedas* laid the groundwork for the richly embellished narratives of later *Itihāsa*, *Purāṇas*, and regional traditions. As we trace these themes into subsequent texts, the concepts of curses and boons will evolve into vivid mythic episodes, yet their essential metaphysical core the belief in the transformative power of sacred speech and its alignment with universal law remains unchanged.

❑

Chapter IV

Thematic Analysis in the Epics *Rāmāyaṇa* and *Mahābhārata*

Within the grand design of the *Rāmāyaṇa* and the *Mahābhārata*, both are revered as *Itihāsas* (historical narratives), the dialectical forces of *śāpa* (curse) and *vara* (boon) operate as crucial narrative devices that structure plot progression, influence character development, and elucidate the moral as well as the cosmic dimensions of *dharma*. These epics inherit the metaphysical framework of the *Vedas*, transforming the potency of spoken words into vivid episodes where curses and boons act as instruments of karmic consequence, moral testing, and spiritual instruction. This chapter undertakes a thematic analysis of key incidents involving *śāpa* and *vara*, examining their role in plot progression, character development, and the ethical architecture of the texts, with a focus on notable examples: Śaṅkara's boon to Rāvaṇa, Kaikeyī's boon, Karna's curse, Gāndhārī's curse, and Śabarī's boon.

Key Incidents of Curses and Boons in the Epics

The *Rāmāyaṇa* and *Mahābhārata* are abound with instances of *śāpa* and *vara*, each serving as a catalyst for narrative momentum and moral exploration. In the

Rāmāyaṇa, boons often elevate or endanger characters, while curses precipitate trials that lead to redemption. For example, Śaṅkara's boon to Rāvaṇa grants him near-invincibility, setting the stage for the epic's central conflict, while Śabarī's boon ensures her liberation through devotion to Rāma. In the *Mahābhārata*, curses and boons are deeply tied to the complexities of *dharma*, driving the tragic arcs of characters like Karna and the catastrophic consequences of Gāndhārī's curse. Bhīṣma's boon of *icchāmṛtyu* (death at will), granted by his father Śantanu, exemplifies the moral burden of divine favours. These incidents, rooted in the spiritual authority of gods, sages, and righteous beings, reveal the profound consequences of actions within the framework of cosmic justice.

Impact on Plot Progression and Character Arcs

In both epics, *śāpa* and *vara* act as narrative fulcrums, steering plots toward climactic resolutions and shaping the destinies of characters. A *vara* often empowers its recipient, but its misuse or unintended consequences can unravel their fortunes, as seen in Rāvaṇa's downfall despite his boon. Conversely, a *śāpa* imposes suffering or limitation, yet it frequently carries the seed of redemption, compelling characters to confront their flaws or fulfill their *dharma*. These acts drive plot progression by introducing conflict, testing resolve, and facilitating transformation, while deepening character arcs by exposing their strengths, vulnerabilities, and moral choices. In the *Rāmāyaṇa*, *śāpa* and *vara* structure the narrative around Rāma's exile and triumph, reinforcing the victory of dharma over *adharma*. In the *Mahābhārata*, their multiplicity reflects the epic's moral ambiguity, where characters grapple with ethical dilemmas and the consequences of their actions, interweaving personal destiny with cosmic causality.

Notable Examples

Śaṅkara's Boon to Rāvaṇa (*Rāmāyaṇa*)

In Vālmīki's *Rāmāyaṇa*, Rāvaṇa, the demon-king of Laṅkā, performs intense austerities to propitiate Lord Śiva (Śaṅkara). Pleased by his devotion, Śiva grants Rāvaṇa a *vara* of invincibility against gods, demons, and celestial beings, though Rāvaṇa, in his hubris, omits mortals from his request. This boon propels the *Rāmāyaṇa's* central conflict, as Rāvaṇa's perceived invulnerability emboldens him to abduct Sītā, setting the stage for his confrontation with Rāma, a mortal incarnation of Viṣṇu. The *vara* shapes Rāvaṇa's character arc, highlighting his arrogance and ultimate downfall, as his boon, while granting immense power, leaves him vulnerable to human agency. This episode illustrates the paradox of boons: they amplify potential but demand wisdom to wield responsibly.

Kaikeyī's Boon (*Rāmāyaṇa*)

Kaikeyī, a beloved queen of Daśaratha, receives two varas from her husband in gratitude for her aid in a past battle. Manipulated by her maid Mantharā, Kaikeyī invokes these boons to demand Rāma's exile for fourteen years and Bharata's ascension to the throne. This pivotal *vara* drives the *Rāmāyaṇa's* plot, thrusting Rāma into exile, triggering Sītā's abduction, and setting the stage for the epic's climactic war. Kaikeyī's arc transforms from a loving mother to a figure of tragic ambition, her boon revealing the destructive potential of desire when divorced from *dharma*. The narrative underscores how a *vara*, though granted in good faith, can disrupt familial harmony and alter destinies when misused.

Karna's Curse (*Mahābhārata*)

Karna, the tragic hero of the *Mahābhārata*, faces multiple curses that shape his doomed fate. A significant śāpa comes from a Brahmin whose cow Karna accidentally kills, cursing him to be helpless at a critical moment in battle, his chariot wheel stuck in the earth. Another curse, from his guru Paraśurāma, strips Karna of his knowledge of divine weapons when he needs it most, as punishment for concealing his non-Brahmin lineage. These curses propel Karna's arc toward tragedy, highlighting his nobility juxtaposed against relentless misfortunes. The *śāpa* underscores the consequences of unintentional errors and societal prejudice, culminating in Karna's death during the Kurukṣetra war, where both curses manifest, sealing his fate.

Gāndhārī's Curse (*Mahābhārata*)

Gāndhārī, the grief-stricken queen of Hastināpura, unleashes a devastating *śāpa* upon Kṛṣṇa after the Kurukṣetra war, holding him responsible for the destruction of her Kuru lineage. Cursing Kṛṣṇa's Yādava clan to perish in internecine strife, Gāndhārī's *śāpa* foreshadows their downfall, as described in the *Mauṣala Parva*. This curse drives the post-war narrative and underscores Gāndhārī's transformation from a passive queen to a figure of righteous wrath. It highlights the moral causality of the epic, where even a divine figure like Kṛṣṇa bears the consequences of cosmic balance, affirming the inevitability of karma.

Śabarī's Boon (*Rāmāyaṇa*)

Śabarī, a humble devotee of Rāma, receives a *vara* from her guru, Sage Mātaṅga, that she will attain liberation upon meeting Rāma. In the Rāmāyaṇa's *Araṇya Kāṇḍa*, Śabarī's unwavering devotion culminates in her encounter with Rāma, who accepts her offerings and grants her *mokṣa*. This *vara* shapes Śabarī's arc as one of pure devotion, elevating her from a marginalized tribal woman to a symbol of spiritual triumph. The boon reinforces Rāma's divine compassion and the accessibility of *dharma* to all, regardless of caste or status, exemplifying the redemptive power of *vara* through faith and humility.

Conclusion

The *Rāmāyaṇa* and *Mahābhārata* illuminate the profound roles of *śāpa* and *vara* as narrative and moral forces, driving plot progression and shaping character arcs with unparalleled depth. From Śaṅkara's boon to Rāvaṇa, which ignites the *Rāmāyaṇa's* central conflict, to Gāndhārī's curse, which seals the tragic fate of the Yādavas, these incidents underscore the interplay of power, responsibility, and cosmic justice. Kaikeyī's boon reveals the perils of desire, Karna's curses highlight the tragedy of unfulfilled potential, and Śabarī's boon celebrates the transformative power of devotion. As these epics expand the Vedic framework of *vāk* into morally charged episodes, they weave a narrative tapestry that reflects the eternal dance of *dharma* and *karma*, inviting readers to contemplate the delicate balance between human choice and divine will. As we progress to the *Purāṇas*, these themes evolve further, enriching India's mythic consciousness with timeless lessons of consequence and redemption.

❑

Chapter V

Boons and Curses in the *Rāmāyaṇa*

In the timeless epic of the *Rāmāyaṇa*, the interplay of boons (*varadāna*) and curses (*śāpa*) predict a complex system that shapes the destinies of gods, mortals, and demons alike. These divine interventions, bestowed as rewards for virtuous deeds or punishments for transgressions, are not mere narrative devices but pivotal forces that steer the course of the epic's events. With a language suffused with grace and grandeur, the *Rāmāyaṇa* illustrates how these celestial pronouncements, rooted in the moral and spiritual ethos of ancient India, alter the lives of its characters, giving rise to moments of triumph, tragedy, and transformation. This chapter explores some of the most significant boons and curses in Vālmīki's *Rāmāyaṇa*, revealing their profound impact on the epic's narrative arc.

The Curse of the Krauñca Birds in Vālmīki's *Rāmāyaṇa*

In the sacred motif of Vālmīki's *Rāmāyaṇa*, where divine boons (*varadāna*) and curses (*śāpa*) weave the threads of destiny, the tale of the Niṣāda hunter and the krauñca birds stands as a luminous prelude. This poignant episode, nestled in the *Bālakāṇḍa*, is not merely a narrative of loss but the very genesis of poetic expression, born from compassion and sorrow. It is here that Sage Vālmīki, moved by the anguish of a grieving bird, utters the first *śloka*, a curse that resonates with the eternal rhythm of *dharma*. This chapter explores this profound moment, where a hunter's act and a sage's empathy give rise to the *Rāmāyaṇa* itself.

The Tragic Fate of the Krauñca Birds

As Sage Vālmīki wandered along the serene banks of the Tamasā river, his heart attuned to the beauty of the forest, he beheld a pair of krauñca birds (cranes), their love a tender dance of devotion. The male and female, entwined in joyous harmony, filled the air with their melodious calls, a living ode to creation's bliss. Vālmīki, enraptured by their bond, paused to witness this embodiment of love and unity.

Yet, in an instant, this idyllic scene was shattered. A Niṣāda hunter, stealthy and unmindful of the sanctity of life, drew his bow and struck the male krauñca with a deadly arrow. The bird fell, its lifeblood staining the earth, its cries silenced forever. The female krauñca, overcome with grief, wailed in heart-rending sorrow, her plaintive cries piercing the forest's tranquility. Her anguish, raw and unbridled, echoed the universal pain of loss, stirring Vālmīki's soul to its depths.

The Birth of the *Śloka* and the Curse

Moved by compassion (*karuṇā*) for the bereaved female krauñca, Vālmīki's heart swelled with righteous indignation. From the depths of his sorrow, words surged forth, unbidden yet perfectly formed, in a rhythm that mirrored the bird's lament. He pronounced a curse upon the Niṣāda hunter in the form of a poetic *śloka*, the first of its kind:

mā niṣāda pratiṣṭhāṃ tvamagamaḥ śāśvatīḥ samāḥ |
yat krauñcamithunādekamavadhīḥ kāmamohitam ||

("O Niṣāda, may you find no peace for endless years, for you have slain one of the krauñca pair, consumed by love.")

This verse, born from Vālmīki's *śoka* (sorrow), became the *śloka* (verse), its metrical cadence a divine gift that would shape the *Rāmāyaṇa's* composition. The curse, while condemning the hunter's cruel act, was not merely punitive; it was an expression of universal compassion, lamenting the disruption of love and harmony. The *śāpa* carried the weight of *dharma*, chastising the hunter for violating the sanctity of life and love.

The Divine Inspiration

As Vālmīki reflected on his spontaneous utterance, Lord Brahmā, the creator, appeared before him, affirming the divine origin of his words. Brahmā revealed that the *śloka* was inspired by divine will, intended to narrate the glorious tale of Śrī Rāma. He bestowed upon Vālmīki a *varadāna*: the ability to perceive Rāma's life in its entirety, from his divine birth to his triumph over Rāvaṇa, and to compose it in the same poetic meter born of the krauñca's sorrow. This boon transformed Vālmīki into the *Ādi Kavi* (first poet), and his Rāmāyaṇa became the eternal epic, its verses flowing like the Tamasā, carrying the essence of *dharma* and devotion.

The curse on the Niṣāda, though directed at a single act, transcended its immediate context. It symbolized the broader moral framework of the *Rāmāyaṇa*, where actions against love, truth, and righteousness invite retribution, while compassion and divine grace pave the path to redemption. The krauñca episode thus serves as the poetic and spiritual foundation of the epic, linking human emotion with cosmic purpose.

The tale of the Niṣāda and the krauñca birds is a luminous gem in the *Rāmāyaṇa*, where a curse born of sorrow gives birth to the sublime art of poetry. Vālmīki's *mā niṣāda* verse, steeped in compassion and *dharma*, not only condemns the hunter's cruelty but also heralds the creation of the śloka meter, through which the epic's timeless narrative unfolds. Coupled with Brahmā's *varadāna*, this episode reveals the *Rāmāyaṇa's* profound truth: even in moments of loss and retribution, divine inspiration can transform pain into beauty, weaving a saga that resonates across ages with the eternal rhythms of love, justice, and redemption.

Śravaṇa Kumāra's Parents' Curse on Daśaratha

One of the most heart-wrenching episodes in the *Rāmāyaṇa* is the tragic curse pronounced upon King Daśaratha, father of Śrī Rāma, which sets the stage for the epic's central exile. Daśaratha, renowned for his mastery of *śabda-bhedī* (sound-guided archery), once ventured into a forest to hunt. Hearing the sound of water being drawn from a river, he mistook it for an animal and released his deadly arrow. To his horror, the arrow struck Śravaṇa Kumāra, a young ascetic fetching water for his blind parents. As Śravaṇa lay dying, he revealed his duty to his elderly parents, urging Daśaratha to inform them of his unintended sin.

When Daśaratha, consumed by guilt, conveyed the tragic news to Śravaṇa's grieving parents, their sorrow turned to wrath. In their anguish, they pronounced a devastating *śāpa*: "As we perish in the agony of separation from our son, so too shall you die in the torment of separation from your son." This curse, born of a parent's unredeemable loss, became the catalyst for Daśaratha's eventual demise. Years later, when Śrī Rāma was exiled due to Kaikeyī's machinations, Daśaratha succumbed to the unbearable pain of separation, fulfilling the curse and underscoring the inexorable power of a righteous *śāpa*.

Tārā's Curse on Śrī Rāma

The *Rāmāyaṇa* also presents a poignant curse directed at Śrī Rāma himself, stemming from his slaying of Vāli, the vānara king. To aid his ally Sugrīva, Rāma struck Vāli with an arrow from a hidden vantage point, an act that sparked controversy for its apparent breach of dharma. Vāli's wife, Tārā, overwhelmed by grief, cursed Rāma with prophetic fury: "Even after regaining your wife, you shall live in the agony of her separation, and in your next birth, my husband shall slay you." This *śāpa* reverberates beyond the *Rāmāyaṇa* into the *Mahābhārata*, where Śrī Kṛṣṇa, believed to be Viṣṇu's incarnation after Rāma, meets his end at the hands of a hunter, said to be Vāli reborn. Tārā's curse thus illustrates the complex interplay of *dharma* and retribution, highlighting how even divine figures are not immune to the consequences of their actions.

The Curse on Hanumān

Hanumān, the devoted follower of Śrī Rāma, is another figure touched by a *śāpa* that shapes his journey. In his youth, Hanumān was a mischievous child endowed with extraordinary powers, including the ability to fly. His playful antics, however, disturbed the meditations of forest sages (*ṛṣis*). Enraged, the sages cursed him: "You shall forget your divine powers until someone reminds you of them." This *śāpa* rendered Hanumān unaware of his own strength until, during the quest to find Sītā, Jāmbavān, the bear king, reminded him of his latent abilities. Empowered by this revelation, Hanumān soared across the ocean to Laṅkā, embodying the transformative potential of overcoming a curse through divine purpose. This episode underscores the notion that a *śāpa* can serve as a temporary veil, lifted when destiny demands.

The Boon of Ṛṣyaśṛṅga and Śāntā

In contrast to the destructive power of curses, boons in the *Rāmāyaṇa* often bring salvation and prosperity. A notable example is the story of Ṛṣyaśṛṅga, the son of Sage Vibhāṇḍaka, and Śāntā, the adopted daughter of King Romapāda. Romapāda's kingdom, Aṅga, suffered a devastating famine as a consequence of his past sins. Seeking a remedy, his council of learned brāhmaṇas advised him to bring Ṛṣyaśṛṅga, a pure and ascetic youth, to the kingdom and wed him to Śāntā, who was originally Daśaratha's daughter, given to Romapāda in adoption. The brāhmaṇas warned, however, that Vibhāṇḍaka might curse anyone who attempted to lure his son, as Ṛṣyaśṛṅga had been sheltered from worldly influences.

To achieve this, Romapāda employed a stratagem, sending beautiful courtesans to entice the innocent Ṛṣyaśṛṅga. Captivated by their charm and unfamiliar with human companionship, Ṛṣyaśṛṅga followed them to Aṅga. As he journeyed along the Gaṅgā, Indra, moved by the sage's purity, showered rain upon the parched land, ending the famine. Upon his arrival, Romapāda welcomed Ṛṣyaśṛṅga and sought a varadāna from him: that neither he nor his father would curse the kingdom for the deception. Ṛṣyaśṛṅga graciously granted this boon, and his marriage to Śāntā was celebrated with great splendor, restoring prosperity to Aṅga. This tale exemplifies how a varadāna can counteract the effects of past misdeeds, bringing harmony and abundance.

The Boon to Nala and Nīla

The *Rāmāyaṇa* also celebrates the boons granted to the vānara brothers Nala and Nīla, whose contributions were vital to the construction of the Rāma-setu (bridge to Laṅkā). According to the epic, Nala, son of Viśvakarmā, the divine architect, received a varadāna from his father that endowed him with unparalleled engineering skills. Similarly, Nīla, blessed by the ocean deity Varuṇa, gained the ability to make stones float on water. These divine gifts enabled the vānara army to construct the miraculous bridge across the ocean, allowing Rāma and his forces to reach Laṅkā and rescue Sītā. The boons bestowed upon Nala and Nīla highlight the *Rāmāyaṇa's* recurring theme of divine favour rewarding skill and devotion, facilitating the triumph of righteousness.

The Curse of Ahalyā

Another profound instance of a *śāpa* is the curse on Ahalyā, the wife of Sage Gautama. Seduced by Indra, who disguised himself as her husband, Ahalyā was cursed by the enraged Gautama to turn into a stone until Śrī Rāma's touch would redeem her. This *śāpa* not only punished Ahalyā but also served as a cautionary tale about fidelity and divine justice. Years later, when Rāma, accompanied by Lakṣmaṇa and Viśvāmitra, touched the stone with his foot, Ahalyā was liberated. Thus, her penance was completed. This episode illustrates the redemptive power of divine grace, where a curse, though severe, can pave the way for spiritual restoration.

The Boon of Kaikeyī

The *Rāmāyaṇa* also features boons that precipitate dramatic turns in the narrative, such as those granted to Kaikeyī by Daśaratha. During a battle in his youth, Kaikeyī, then Daśaratha's wife, saved his life by skillfully steering his chariot to safety. In gratitude, Daśaratha promised her two *varadānas*, to be fulfilled at her discretion. Years later, influenced by her maid Mantharā, Kaikyī invoked these boons to demand Rāma's exile for fourteen years and the coronation of her son, Bharata. This act, though driven by personal ambition, fulfilled the divine plan to orchestrate Rāma's journey to slay Rāvaṇa, demonstrating how even seemingly malevolent boons can serve a higher cosmic purpose.

The Curse on Kākabhūṣaṇḍi

One intriguing tale involves Kākabhūṣaṇḍi, a sage who, in a previous life as a devotee, incurred the wrath of Lord Śiva. According to the *Rāmāyaṇa* (as elaborated in later retellings like the *Adhyātma Rāmāyaṇa*), Kākabhūṣaṇḍi, then a brāhmaṇa, was an ardent devotee of Śiva but disrespected Lord Viṣṇu, considering him inferior. Offended by this hubris, Śiva cursed him: "You shall be reborn as a crow, wandering the earth until you realize the unity of all divine forms." This *śāpa* transformed the brāhmaṇa into Kākabhūṣaṇḍi, the crow sage, destined to narrate the *Rāmāyaṇa* to future generations. However, the curse was tempered by a *varadāna* from Śiva: Kākabhūṣaṇḍi would gain eternal wisdom and devotion to Śrī Rāma, becoming a timeless storyteller of his divine exploits. This tale illustrates how a curse, born of pride, can lead to spiritual redemption through divine grace, as Kākabhūṣaṇḍi's crow form allowed him to witness and share Rāma's glory across eons.

The Boon to Rāvaṇa

The mighty demon king Rāvaṇa, central to the *Rāmāyaṇa's* conflict, owed his formidable power to a *varadāna* from Lord Brahmā. In his quest for invincibility, Rāvaṇa performed intense austerities (*tapas*) to please Brahmā. Pleased by his devotion, Brahmā granted him a boon: immunity from death at the hands of gods, demons, gandharvas, yakṣas, and other celestial beings. Arrogantly, Rāvaṇa omitted humans and monkeys from his request, deeming them insignificant. This *varadāna* made Rāvaṇa nearly invincible, fueling his tyranny and eventual abduction of Sītā. Yet, it also sowed the seeds of his downfall, as Śrī Rāma, a human, and his *vānara* allies, led by Sugrīva and Hanumān, were not bound by the boon's protection. Rāvaṇa's story highlights the double-edged nature of boons, where divine favour, when coupled with hubris, can lead to ruin.

Vāli's Boon and Tārā's Curse

Vāli, the mighty king of the *vānara* kingdom of Kiṣkindhā, was endowed with a formidable *varadāna* that made him a near-invincible warrior. According to the *Rāmāyaṇa*, Vāli performed intense austerities (*tapas*) to please Lord Brahmā, who granted him a unique boon: in any duel, Vāli would absorb half the strength of his opponent, rendering him virtually unbeatable. This *varadāna* fueled Vāli's confidence and dominance, enabling him to defeat powerful foes, including the demon Dundubhi, whose corpse he hurled across vast distances as a display of prowess. However, this boon also sowed the seeds of his hubris, leading to his estrangement from his brother Sugrīva, who sought Śrī Rāma's aid to reclaim the throne.

When Śrī Rāma, upholding his alliance with Sugrīva, slew Vāli from a hidden vantage point an act debated for its adherence to *dharma* Vāli's wife, Tārā, was consumed by grief and rage. In her anguish, she pronounced a *śāpa* upon Rāma: "Even after regaining your wife, you shall live in the agony of separation from her, and in your next birth, my husband shall slay you." This curse, born of a widow's sorrow, reverberated beyond the *Rāmāyaṇa*. In the *Mahābhārata*, Śrī Kṛṣṇa, considered Viṣṇu's incarnation after Rāma, meets his end at the hands of a hunter, believed to be Vāli reborn. Vāli's boon and Tārā's curse thus illustrate the dual nature of divine gifts and retribution, where power granted by a boon can lead to pride and a curse can foreshadow cosmic justice across lifetimes.

The Curse on Nārada and Viṣṇu's Boon

The sage Nārada, known for his wisdom and devotion, features in a lesser-known episode involving a curse and a subsequent boon that, indirectly influences the *Rāmāyaṇa*. In a past incident, Nārada, enamoured by his own beauty, sought to marry a princess during a *svayaṃvara*. To ensure his success, he requested Lord Viṣṇu to grant him a divine appearance. Viṣṇu, in a playful yet instructive act, gave Nārada the face of a monkey. Unaware of his altered visage, Nārada attended the *svayaṃvara*, only to be mocked and rejected. Infuriated, Nārada cursed Viṣṇu: "You shall take a human form and rely on monkeys to accomplish your divine mission." Viṣṇu, smiling, accepted the curse and granted Nārada a varadāna of unwavering devotion to him. This curse manifested in Viṣṇu's incarnation as Śrī Rāma, who allied with the *vānara* army to defeat Rāvaṇa, while Nārada's boon ensured his eternal role as a devotee and narrator of divine tales. This episode proves the interplay of divine jest, retribution, and redemption.

The Curse on King Pratāpabhānu

In some regional retellings of the *Rāmāyaṇa*, such as the *Adhyātma Rāmāyaṇa*, the story of King Pratāpabhānu illustrates how a curse can precipitate cosmic events. Pratāpabhānu, a righteous king, was once deceived by a cunning sage who, envious of his prosperity, tricked him into offending brāhmaṇas by serving them forbidden meat during a feast. Outraged, the brāhmaṇas cursed him: "You shall be reborn as a demon, and your lineage will face destruction." This śāpa led to Pratāpabhānu's rebirth as Rāvaṇa, whose actions set the stage for the *Rāmāyaṇa's* central conflict. However, the curse was mitigated by a *varadāna* from a compassionate sage, who promised that Pratāpabhānu's soul would be liberated by Viṣṇu's incarnation. Thus, Rāvaṇa's death at Rāma's hands was not merely defeat but a path to *mokṣa*, illustrating how curses can serve as instruments of divine justice and ultimate salvation.

The Boon to Sugrīva

Sugrīva, the exiled vānara king, received a significant *varadāna* that bolstered his role in the *Rāmāyaṇa*. After forming an alliance with Śrī Rāma, Sugrīva was blessed by sages and divine forces for his loyalty and devotion. According to some accounts, he received a boon of enhanced strength and leadership, enabling him to rally the *vānara* army and assist Rāma in his quest to rescue Sītā. This *varadāna* not only restored Sugrīva's kingdom after Vāli's death but also cemented his place as a key ally in the battle against Rāvaṇa. The boon reflects the *Rāmāyaṇa's* theme of divine favour rewarding fidelity and courage, ensuring that those who uphold dharma are empowered to fulfill their roles in the cosmic order.

The Curse on Jāmbavān's Daughter

In a lesser-known tale, Jāmbavān, the wise bear king, faced a familial curse that added depth to his character. His daughter, Jāmbavatī, is said to have once disturbed a sage's penance through her playful antics. The sage, in anger, cursed her: "You shall marry a human and live apart from your kind." This *śāpa* later manifested when Jāmbavatī married Śrī Kṛṣṇa (Viṣṇu's incarnation after Rāma) in the *Mahābhārata*. However, the sage, moved by Jāmbavān's plea, granted a *varadāna* that Jāmbavatī's union would be with a divine being, ensuring her honour and happiness. In the *Rāmāyaṇa*, Jāmbavān's wisdom and strength, possibly bolstered by his own past boons, enabled him to guide Hanumān and the *vānara* army, indirectly linking this curse to the epic's narrative.

The Boon to Vibhīṣaṇa

Vibhīṣaṇa, Rāvaṇa's righteous brother, received a *varadāna* that distinguished him from his demon king. During Rāvaṇa's penance to Brahmā, Vibhīṣaṇa sought a boon of unwavering devotion to *dharma* and Viṣṇu. Brahmā granted this, ensuring that Vibhīṣaṇa's heart remained pure despite his demonic lineage. This boon guided his decision to abandon Rāvaṇa and join Śrī Rāma, earning him the kingship of Laṅkā after Rāvaṇa's defeat. Vibhīṣaṇa's *varadāna* exemplifies how divine favour can elevate a character above their circumstances, aligning them with righteousness and ensuring their triumph in the face of adversity.

The Curse on the Gandharva Virādha

In the *Araṇyakāṇḍa* of the *Rāmāyaṇa*, Śrī Rāma and Lakṣmaṇa encounter the monstrous gandharva Virādha, who attempts to abduct Sītā in the Daṇḍaka forest. Virādha, originally a celestial gandharva named Tumburu, was cursed by his master, the sage Kubera, for neglecting his duties in favour of indulging in amorous pursuits with the apsara Rambhā. The *śāpa* transformed Tumburu into a fearsome rākṣasa, doomed to roam the forest until he was slain by a divine being. Kubera, however, mitigated the curse with a varadāna: Tumburu would be liberated from his monstrous form upon death at the hands of Śrī Rāma. When Rāma and Lakṣmaṇa defeat Virādha, his true gandharva form is restored, and he ascends to the heavens, praising Rāma's divine grace. This episode illustrates how a curse, though punitive, can serve as a path to redemption when intertwined with divine intervention.

The Boon to Śabarī

Śabarī, the humble ascetic woman who devotedly awaited Śrī Rāma in the forest, is another recipient of a divine varadāna that shapes her role in the *Rāmāyaṇa*. A disciple of Sage Mātaṅga, Śabarī belonged to a tribal community but dedicated her life to spiritual practice. Pleased by her unwavering devotion and service, Mātaṅga granted her a boon before his death: "You shall behold Śrī Rāma in this very *āśrama*, and his *darśana* will grant you liberation." This varadāna sustained Śabarī through years of solitude, as she maintained Mātaṅga's hermitage, collecting fruits for Rāma's arrival. When Rāma and Lakṣmaṇa finally visited, Śabarī offered them hospitality with profound love, tasted the fruits to ensure their sweetness, and, upon receiving

Rāma's blessings, attained mokṣa. Śabarī's story highlights how a boon can reward steadfast devotion, transforming a humble life into one of divine fulfillment.

The Curse on Kabandha

Another striking tale involves Kabandha, a grotesque rākṣasa encountered by Rāma and Lakṣmaṇa in the forest. Originally a gandharva named Danu, Kabandha was cursed by a sage (or, in some versions, by Indra) for his arrogance and misdeeds. The śāpa distorted him into a headless creature with a single eye and arms stretching a yojana, condemned to a life of terror until he was slain by a divine incarnation. The curse was softened by a *varadāna* that his liberation would come through Śrī Rāma. When Rāma and Lakṣmaṇa dismember and cremate Kabandha, he regains his celestial form and, in gratitude, advises Rāma to ally with Sugrīva, thus aiding the quest for Sītā. Kabandha's tale pinpoints the *Rāmāyaṇa's* recurring motif of curses as transformative trials, leading to salvation through divine encounter.

The Boon to Sampāti

Sampāti, the elder brother of Jaṭāyu, plays a crucial role in guiding the vānara search party to Sītā's location in Laṅkā. His story is tied to a curse and a subsequent boon. In their youth, Sampāti and Jaṭāyu, both mighty vultures, competed to fly toward the sun. Sampāti, protecting his younger brother from the sun's scorching heat, burned his wings and fell to the earth. A sage (or, in some versions, the sun god Sūrya), moved by his sacrifice, cursed him for his hubris in challenging the sun but granted a *varadāna*: "You shall regain your strength and purpose when you aid Śrī Rāma's cause." Years later, when the *vānara* search party reached the southern shore, Sampāti, now old and wingless, shared vital information about Sītā's captivity in Laṅkā. His wings miraculously regenerated, fulfilling the boon and enabling him to soar once more. Sampāti's story reflects the redemptive power of selflessness, rewarded through divine favour.

The Curse on the Apsara Urvaśī and Its Impact on Arjuna

While primarily a *Mahābhārata* figure, Arjuna's connection to the *Rāmāyaṇa* emerges through a curse involving the apsara Urvaśī, which some retellings link to Rāma's narrative. Urvaśī, enamoured with Arjuna (believed to be an incarnation of Viṣṇu, like Rāma), proposed him in Indra's court. Arjuna, respecting her as a maternal figure, declined. Enraged, Urvaśī cursed him: "You shall live as a eunuch among women." Indra, softening the *śāpa*, granted a *varadāna* that this curse would last only a year, serving Arjuna's purpose during the Pāṇḍavas' exile. In some interpretations, this curse is seen as a karmic echo of Rāma's trials, as both Viṣṇu's incarnations faced challenges tied to separation and duty. While tangential, this story connects the *Rāmāyaṇa's* themes of divine curses and boons to the broader Indian mythological tradition.

The Boon to Maṇḍodarī

Maṇḍodarī, Rāvaṇa's virtuous wife, is indirectly associated with a *varadāna* that highlights her righteousness. In some versions of the *Rāmāyaṇa*, Maṇḍodarī, a devotee of Śiva or Viṣṇu, was blessed with a boon of spiritual wisdom, enabling her to recognize Rāvaṇa's impending doom and counsel him against abducting Sītā. Though her advice went unheeded, this *varadāna* ensured her protection and honour after Rāvaṇa's death. When Śrī Rāma defeated Rāvaṇa, Maṇḍodarī was spared and revered for her piety, later living under Vibhīṣaṇa's rule in Laṅkā. Her boon highlights the *Rāmāyaṇa's* emphasis on righteousness prevailing, even in the midst of chaos, and the protective power of divine favour.

Kumbhakarṇa's Boon and Curse

Kumbhakarṇa, the colossal brother of Rāvaṇa, is a figure whose fate in the *Rāmāyaṇa* is profoundly shaped by a boon and a curse-like twist of divine will. A rākṣasa of immense strength and loyalty, Kumbhakarṇa joined his brothers Rāvaṇa and Vibhīṣaṇa in performing rigorous austerities (*tapas*) to please Lord Brahmā. When Brahmā appeared, ready to grant a *varadāna*, Kumbhakarṇa intended to request nirdevatvam (dominion over the gods). However, the goddess Sarasvatī, fearing his potential for destruction, intervened by confounding his speech. Instead of nirdevatvam, Kumbhakarṇa uttered *nidrāvatvam* (eternal sleep), a slip orchestrated by divine will. Brahmā granted this boon, decreeing that Kumbhakarṇa would sleep for six months at a time, waking only briefly to consume vast quantities of food before returning to slumber.

This *varadāna*, though seemingly a curse due to its limiting nature, was a divine safeguard to curb Kumbhakarṇa's might, which could have rivaled Rāvaṇa's tyranny. When Rāvaṇa summoned him during the war against Śrī Rāma, Kumbhakarṇa, awakened from his slumber, fought valiantly but met his end at Rāma's hands. In some interpretations, his death is seen as a liberation, as his loyalty to his brother was tempered by his recognition of

Rāvaṇa's adharma. Kumbhakarṇa's story illustrates how a boon, altered by divine intervention, can serve as a cosmic check on power, aligning his fate with the greater purpose of upholding righteousness.

Lakṣmaṇa's Curse by Sage Durvāsā

Lakṣmaṇa, the devoted brother of Śrī Rāma, is rarely associated with curses in the *Rāmāyaṇa*, as his life is marked by unwavering loyalty and *dharma*. However, in some regional retellings and later interpolations, such as those found in the *Adhyātma Rāmāyaṇa* or folk traditions, Lakṣmaṇa is linked to a minor yet significant *śāpa* from Sage Durvāsā. During Rāma's exile, while guarding the hut where Rāma and Sītā resided, Lakṣmaṇa was approached by Durvāsā, who demanded an audience with Rāma. Bound by Rāma's instruction to allow no interruptions during a confidential meeting with a divine emissary (often Yama, the god of death, in disguise), Lakṣmaṇa hesitated. Durvāsā, known for his fiery temper, cursed Lakṣmaṇa: "For obstructing a sage's will, you shall face separation from your beloved brother in this life."

This *śāpa* is said to have manifested subtly, as Lakṣmaṇa endured moments of emotional separation from Rāma, particularly during Sītā's abduction and Rāma's moments of despair. However, the curse was mitigated by Rāma's divine grace and Lakṣmaṇa's unyielding devotion. In some versions, Durvāsā, moved by Lakṣmaṇa's apology, granted a varadāna that his loyalty would earn him eternal fame as the ideal brother and devotee. While not a central episode in Vālmīki's *Rāmāyaṇa*, this tale reflects the theme of curses as tests of virtue, with Lakṣmaṇa's steadfastness transforming a potential punishment into a testament to his *dharma*.

The Boon to Lakṣmaṇa

Lakṣmaṇa also received divine boons that bolstered his role as Rāma's protector. In the *Rāmāyaṇa*, sages and celestial beings, recognizing Lakṣmaṇa's selfless service, blessed him with extraordinary strength and resilience. During the exile, Sage Viśvāmitra, who had earlier guided Rāma, is said to have granted Lakṣmaṇa a *varadāna* of unmatched prowess in battle, particularly in archery and close combat. This boon enabled Lakṣmaṇa to confront formidable foes like Indrajit, Rāvaṇa's son, and protect Rāma and Sītā throughout their trials. Additionally, in some versions, the gods bestowed upon Lakṣmaṇa the blessing of tirelessness, allowing him to remain vigilant during his fourteen-year vigil guarding Rāma and Sītā, notably during his refusal to sleep while protecting Sītā in the forest. These *varadānas* highlight Lakṣmaṇa's role as the embodiment of loyalty and sacrifice, ensuring his contributions to Rāma's mission were divinely empowered.

Indrajit's Boons and Their Consequences

Indrajit, the formidable son of Rāvaṇa, also known as Meghanāda, was a warrior whose prowess rivaled the gods themselves, owing to powerful *varadānas* he secured through intense penance. Born to Rāvaṇa and Maṇḍodarī, Meghanāda earned his name "Indrajit" (Conqueror of Indra) by defeating the king of gods in battle, a feat made possible by divine boons. According to the *Rāmāyaṇa*, Indrajit performed rigorous tapas to propitiate Lord Brahmā, who granted him two significant *varadānas*. The first was a celestial chariot (*ratha*), invisible to enemies and drawn by divine horses, which rendered him nearly invincible in battle. The second boon endowed him with mastery over the

Brahmāstra, a weapon of unparalleled destructive power, and the ability to wield illusory tactics (*māyā*), making him a terror on the battlefield.

These boons elevated Indrajit to a near-unassailable status, allowing him to bind Śrī Rāma and Lakṣmaṇa with the *nāgapāśa* (serpent noose) and unleash devastating attacks on the *vānara* army. However, his boons came with a critical limitation: they did not protect him from death if his secret rituals, particularly the Nikumbhilā *yajña*, were interrupted. Lakṣmaṇa, guided by Vibhīṣaṇa, disrupted this sacrificial rite, ultimately leading to Indrajit's demise at Lakṣmaṇa's hands. Indrajit's story emphasises the *Rāmāyaṇa's* theme that even the mightiest boons, when wielded with arrogance or in defiance of *dharma*, cannot defy the cosmic order. His defeat illustrates that divine gifts, while powerful, are bound by the moral constraints of righteousness.

Conclusion

The boons and curses in the *Rāmāyaṇa* are not mere plot devices but profound expressions of *dharma*, *karma*, and divine will. Whether it is the heart-rending curse of Śravaṇa's parents, the redemptive liberation of Ahalyā, or the strategic boons granted to Nala, Nīla, and Ṛṣyaśṛṅga, these divine interventions shape the moral and spiritual landscape of the epic. They remind us that in the cosmic order, every action, be it virtuous or errant carries consequences that ripple through time, weaving a narrative that is as instructive as it is enchanting. Through these stories, the *Rāmāyaṇa* teaches that boons and curses, though bestowed in moments of passion or piety, ultimately serve to uphold the eternal principles of righteousness and justice.

These tales of boons and curses in the *Rāmāyaṇa* weave

a rich mosaic of divine intervention, moral consequence, and spiritual redemption. From Kākabhūṣaṇḍi's transformation into a wise crow to Rāvaṇa's flawed invincibility, and from Nārada's playful curse to Vibhīṣaṇa's righteous boon, each story underscores the epic's central theme: the inexorable interplay of *dharma* and *karma*. These divine pronouncements, whether punitive or benevolent, are not mere whims of fate but purposeful acts that guide the characters toward their destinies, shaping the *Rāmāyaṇa* into a timeless saga of justice, devotion, and cosmic balance.

❑

Chapter VI

Boons and Curses in the *Mahābhārata*: The Cosmic Dance of Divine Will

In the vast carving of the *Mahābhārata*, where gods and mortals are destined through an intricate scheming of *dharma* and *karma*, the phenomena of boons (*vara*) and curses (*śāpa*) act as mysterious threads, stitching together the cosmic drama of human existence. These divine interventions, exhibitted by gods, sages, and celestial beings, are not mere narrative flourishes but pivotal mechanisms that propel the epic's unfolding. Within the *Ādiparva*, the first book of this grand epic, boons and curses act as the silent prompters of fate, orchestrating the rise and fall of heroes, the clash of divine and demonic forces, and the eternal struggle between righteousness and chaos.

The Essence of Boons and Curses

Boons and curses in the *Mahābhārata* are not mere blessings or maledictions but potent acts of divine and human will, charged with the power to alter destinies. A boon, often translated as *vara*, is a divine favour, a gift of grace that can confer prosperity, progeny, or supernatural prowess. A curse, or *śāpa*, is its shadow counterpart, a pronouncement of misfortune that can bind a soul to suffering or transformation. Together, they form a unitary phenomenon, two sides of the same cosmic coin, wielded by beings of immense spiritual authority-gods, *ṛṣis* (sages), and Brahmins who hold sway over the play of existence.

The *Ādiparva*, as Woods notes, is particularly rich in these phenomena, serving as a crucible where the seeds of the epic's grand narrative are sown. Boons and curses are not random; they are deliberate acts, often tied to the moral and spiritual merit of the recipient or the transgression that provokes them. They reflect the interplay of *tapas* (ascetic power), *tejas* (spiritual radiance), and *dharma* (cosmic order), shaping the lives of mortals and immortals alike in a universe where every action ripples across the *lokas* (realms of existence).

The Administration of Divine Will

Who wields the power to grant boons or pronounce curses? In the *Mahābhārata*, this authority rests with beings of elevated spiritual stature. Gods like Brahmā, Viṣṇu, and Śiva, as well as revered sages like Nārada and Vyāsa, are primary dispensers. Woods observes that gods are more likely to bestow boons twenty eight of the fifty seven boons in the *Ādiparva* originate from divine sources while sages, particularly ascetic *ṛṣis*, are prone to cursing, their *śāpas* often born of anger or moral indignation. For instance, the sage Apimāṇḍavya curses the god *Dharma* himself to be born as Vidura in a *śūdra* womb, a punishment for perceived injustice (*Mahābhārata* I.107). This act intensifies the *ṛṣi's tapas-śakti*, enabling him to bind even the *devas* within the contingencies of mortal *karma* and destiny

Mortals, too, can wield this power when imbued with

sufficient merit. Kṣatriyas like Arjuna and Karṇa, through their tapas or divine favour, can curse or bless, as seen when both curse the snake Aśvasena for merely escaping death (*Mahābhārata* I.218.10). The phenomenon transcends rigid hierarchies, reflecting a fluid cosmos where merit, not birth, determines authority. The *Ādiparva's* temporal setting, primarily in the *kṛtayuga* (the golden age), amplifies this power, as divine and human realms interpenetrate, allowing boons and curses to shape the course of the epic across eons.

The Forms and Functions of Boons and Curses

Boons and curses manifest in diverse forms, each tailored to the context of its bestowal. Woods categorizes curses into homoeopathic and heteropathic types. Homoeopathic curses amplify the transgression that provoked them, as when Yayāti's sons are cursed for disobedience, their defiance mirrored in their punishment (*Mahābhārata* I.84). Heteropathic curses, conversely, reverse the circumstances, such as when Indra, boasting of his supremacy, is cursed to be reborn as Arjuna among mortals (*Mahābhārata* I.18.15). Boons, meanwhile, often confer prosperity (artha), progeny, or spiritual power, as seen when Yudhiṣṭhira receives a mantra granting celestial vision (*Mahābhārata* I.126.35).

The "truth command" (*satyavacana*) is a related phenomenon, where the power of truth itself compels reality to bend. For example, a declaration like "If it be true that I recognize no man but the Pāṇḍavas, then by this truth…" (*Mahābhārata* I.18) can effect a boon-like outcome. Oaths and vows, too, carry a curse-like weight when broken, binding the speaker to their word with cosmic consequences.

The motives behind these acts are as varied as their

forms. Boons may stem from devotion, praise, or compassion, as when the Aśvins restore Upamanyu's sight after his hymns of praise (*Mahābhārata* I.3.75). Curses often arise from disobedience or hubris, yet they can also be acts of justice, as when Kadrū's curse on the snakes (*Mahābhārata* I.33.1) sets the stage for their salvation through sacrifice. The psychodynamics of these acts reveal a universe where emotional extremities such as anger, devotion, or charity channel divine power into human affairs.

Narrative Significance: The Prompters of Fate

In the *Mahābhārata*, boons and curses are not mere plot devices but integral to the epic's worldview, serving as the "off-stage prompters" of fate, as Woods eloquently puts it. They orchestrate the cosmic drama, ensuring that dharma prevails despite the chaos of human ambition. The curse of Pāṇḍu, for instance, which prevents him from fathering children directly, necessitates the divine incarnation of the Pāṇḍavas, setting the stage for the epic's central conflict (*Mahābhārata* I.109). Similarly, boons granted by Bhīṣma, Droṇa, and Śalya to the Pāṇḍavas bolster the forces of righteousness, ensuring their eventual triumph.

These phenomena also bridge the microcosm of human life with the macrocosm of divine order. They reflect the tension between *karma* (action) and *daiva* (fate), a central philosophical concern of the epic. While karma suggests that human exertion shapes destiny, boons and curses introduce an element of divine intervention, complicating the doctrine. For instance, the undeserved curse on Aśvasena or the snakes challenges the notion of karmic justice, suggesting that fate sometimes operates beyond human control. Yet, as Woods notes, the epic reconciles these tensions through the concept of divine grace (*prasāda*), which can mitigate curses or amplify boons, as seen when Viṣṇu's intervention softens Garuḍa's fate (*Mahābhārata* I.29).

The Unitary Vision: A Cosmic Synthesis

The *Mahābhārata's* treatment of boons and curses reflects a unitary vision where human and divine realms are intertwined. These acts are not anomalies but expressions of a cosmic order governed by *dharma, tapas*, and the interplay of *guṇas* (*sattva, rajas, tamas*). They accentuate the epic's pessimistic yet hopeful worldview: while humans are bound by the "nooses of fate" (*Mahābhārata* V.50.55), divine grace and individual exertion offer paths to transcendence. The renunciation of action's fruits, as Kṛṣṇa advocates in the *Bhagavadgītā* (VI.28.16-20), emerges as a counterpoint to the deterministic force of boons and curses, suggesting that true liberation lies beyond their sway.

In the *Ādiparva*, boons and curses are the invisible hands that guide the epic's narrative, shaping the destinies of gods, demons, and mortals. They are the sparks that ignite the cosmic drama, the whispers of fate that echo through the ages, reminding us that in the *Mahābhārata's* universe, every act, whether human or divine, is a step in the eternal dance of creation and destruction.

The *Mahābhārata's Vara* and *Śāpa*: Boons and Curses in Sanskrit Thought

In the brilliant picturisation of Indian mythology, the *Mahābhārata* stands as an organice thread, uniting together the cosmic and human realms through the intricate subtle design of boons (*vara*) and curses (*śāpa*). These phenomena are not mere narrative devices but profound expressions of divine and human agency, encapsulating the moral and metaphysical underpinnings of the epic. This chapter delves into the phenomenon of boons and curses, with a specific focus on their Sanskrit terminology, as elucidated in the *Ādiparva* of the *Mahābhārata*. Through an exploration of the linguistic nuances and cultural significance of these terms, we uncover their role as pivotal forces shaping the destinies of gods, sages, and mortals alike.

The Phenomenon of Boons and Curses: A Cosmic Dance

In the *Mahābhārata*, boons and curses are not isolated events but integral components of a cosmic drama, serving as the "prompters" that guide the narrative toward its destined resolution. A boon, or *vara*, is a divine or supernatural favour bestowed upon a recipient, often granting extraordinary powers, longevity, or fulfillment of desires. A curse, or *śāpa*, conversely, imposes a penalty or transformation, redirecting the course of a being's fate, often as a consequence of transgression or hubris. Together, these phenomena reflect the dynamic interplay of *dharma* (cosmic order) and *adharma* (disorder), operating across the kaleidoscopic *lokas* (realms) of the epic's universe.

The *Ādiparva*, the foundational book of the *Mahābhārata*, is particularly rich with instances of boons and curses, offering a fertile ground for examining their phenomenological essence. As noted by scholars like N.C. Kelkar, this section of the epic is a treasure trove of such occurrences, where gods, *ṛṣis* (sages), and mortals engage in a delicate dance of power, merit, and retribution. The phenomenon transcends mere empirical events, embodying a metaphysical framework where human actions intersect with divine will, shaped by the potent force of the spoken word.

The Sanskrit Terminology of "Boon"

The Sanskrit term for a boon, *vara*, is derived from the root *vṛ*, meaning "to choose" or "to select." This etymology imbues *vara* with a sense of deliberate bestowal, a conscious act of granting a favour or privilege. In the *Mahābhārata, vara* is not a casual gift but a sacred transaction, often conferred by deities or enlightened beings such as Brahmā, Viṣṇu, or revered *ṛṣis*. The term encapsulates a spectrum of blessings, from material prosperity (*artha*) and progeny to spiritual ascendancy and liberation.

In the *Ādiparva, vara* manifests in diverse forms. For instance, the boon granted by Brahmā to the Earth, addressing the birth of the *Dānavas* among men, emohasizes its cosmic significance (I.208.20). Similarly, the Ganges' boon to the Vasus reflects a divine intervention in the *dvāparayuga* (I.90.60). The term *vara* is also used interchangeably with other expressions, such as *mantra* (magical spell) or *vidyā* (knowledge), as seen when Yudhiṣṭhira receives a celestial vision through a *mantra* (I.126.35). However, care must be taken to distinguish *vara* from related terms like *prasāda* (divine grace), which carries connotations of unmerited favour, as in the *Bhagavadgītā's* invocation of divine grace to surmount karmic effects (III.81.13).

The bestowal of a *vara* is often conditional, tied to the recipient's merit (*puṇya*) or the grantor's intent. For example, the boon of progeny, a recurring motif, is linked to *artha* and the repayment of ancestral debts (I.14.5; I.78.1). The term's flexibility allows it to encompass both tangible rewards and intangible spiritual gifts, reflecting the Hindu mind's nuanced understanding of divine favour. The power of *vara* lies in its ability to alter destinies, as seen in the case of Arjuna, who receives divine weapons as boons, enabling his role in the epic's cosmic struggle (III.41.5).

The Sanskrit Terminology of "Curse"

The Sanskrit term for a curse, *śāpa*, is derives from the root *śap*, meaning "to curse" or "to swear." This term carries a weight of solemnity, evoking the power of the spoken word to bind or afflict. In the *Mahābhārata, śāpa* is a potent instrument wielded by those with spiritual authority *ṛṣis*, gods, or even mortals with accumulated *tapas* (ascetic power). Unlike *vara*, which elevates, *śāpa* often diminishes, imposing a penalty that ranges from physical transformation to existential suffering.

In the *Ādiparva, śāpa* is frequently associated with *ṛṣis*, whose ascetic prowess makes them formidable dispensers of curses. For instance, the brahmin seer's curse upon an apsara (I.208.20) and Kṛpa's curse on Aśvasena (I.218.10) illustrate the diversity of *śāpa's* application. The term is sometimes conflated with *dhik* (a term of reproach or condemnation), as seen in the cursing of Bhīṣma (I.165.42). However, *śāpa* is distinct in its formalized invocation, often accompanied by a specific formula such as "You shall…" (I.20.15), aligning it with the ritualistic power of mantras or sacrificial rites.

Curses in the *Mahābhārata* are categorized into homoeopathic and heteropathic types. Homoeopathic curses repay in kind, amplifying the transgression, as when Indra is cursed to fall from his divine status for his hubris (I.18.15). Heteropathic curses, conversely, reverse the circumstances, such as the curse on Yayāti's sons for disobedience, transforming their fates dramatically (I.75.10). The term *śāpa* also intersects with related phenomena like vows (*vrata*) and oaths (*śapatha*), which carry conditional penalties, as seen in Bhīma's vow to break his enemy's thigh (II.63.15).

The Interplay of *Vara* and *Śāpa*: A Linguistic and Cultural Synthesis

The Sanskrit terminology of *vara* and *śāpa* reveals a profound cultural synthesis, blending Vedic, magical, and ascetic traditions. The Vedic roots of *vara* and *śāpa* lie in the power of the spoken word, as seen in the *Ṛgveda's* hymns, where *mantras* wield cosmic influence (*Ṛgveda* I.24.9). The magical tradition, formalized in the *Atharvaveda*, imbues these terms with ritual potency, while the ascetic tradition, emphasizing tapas, amplifies their efficacy through spiritual merit. This synthesis is evident in the *Mahābhārata's* portrayal of *ṛṣis* like Nārada, who wield *śāpa* with precision, or gods like Viṣṇu, who grant *vara* to restore cosmic balance.

The linguistic precision of *vara* and *śāpa* underscores their role as instruments of *dharma*. A *vara* aligns with the path of *pravṛtti* (action), propelling the recipient toward their destined role, while a *śāpa* often serves as a corrective, redirecting *adharma* back to the fold of cosmic order. Their interplay reflects the *Mahābhārata's* unitary vision, where human exertion (*puruṣakāra*) and divine destiny (*daiva*) converge. As the epic declares, "The acts, good and bad, that a *jīva* does are not subject to destruction" (III.33.10), highlighting the enduring impact of *vara* and *śāpa* across lifetimes.

Conclusion

In the *Mahābhārata*, *vara* and *śāpa* are more than linguistic constructs; they are the threads that weave the epic's narrative, binding the microcosm of human life to the macrocosm of divine will. The Sanskrit terminology reveals their rootedness in a worldview where words are sacred, capable of shaping destinies and upholding *dharma*. As prompters in the cosmic *drama*, boons and curses orchestrate the interplay of fate and free will, illuminating the eternal quest for meaning in the vicissitudes of existence. Through their evocative power, *vara* and *śāpa* invite us to ponder the delicate balance between human agency and the inexorable tides of destiny, a dance that resonates through the ages in the luminous verses of the *Mahābhārata*.

❑

Chapter VII

Boons and Curses in Sanskrit Classical Literature

Going through the critical viscera of Sanskrit classical literature, boons (*vara*) and curses (*śāpa*) are supposed to be a narrative thread that unites the divine to the mortal, the ethereal to the earthly. These twin forces blessings bestowed by gods or sages and curses hurled in moments of wrath shape destinies, propel plots, and illuminate the moral and spiritual cosmos of Indian mythology. From the lyrical *dramas* of Bhāsa to the ornate *kāvyas* of Kālidāsa, Aśvaghoṣa, Bhāravi, Māgha, and Śrīharṣa, boons and curses are not mere plot devices but profound expressions of *dharma*, *karma*, and the interplay of human agency with cosmic will. Their interplay evokes awe, stirs pathos, and invites contemplation of life's impermanence and the weight of actions. This chapter explores these themes, drawing from the timeless works of these literary giants, where divine gifts and mortal failings dance in eternal rhythm.

The Divine Gift: Vara as Destiny's Pivot

In Sanskrit literature, a *vara* is a divine boon, a celestial favour granted by gods, sages, or supernatural beings, often in response to penance (*tapas*), devotion (*bhakti*), or heroic deeds. These boons are transformative, altering the course of lives and narratives, yet they frequently carry unforeseen consequences, reflecting the ambivalence of divine intervention.

Kālidāsa, the master of poetic elegance, wields boons as instruments of divine grace in his works. In *Abhijñānaśākuntalam*, the sage Durvāsas' curse upon Śakuntalā sets the stage for her tragic separation from King Duṣyanta, but it is the boon of memory restored through the ring that reunites them. The *vara* here is subtle, embedded in the narrative's resolution, where divine intervention corrects the course of human error. Kālidāsa's *Kumārasambhavam* offers a grander canvas: Pārvatī's arduous *tapas* earns her the boon of Śiva's love, culminating in the birth of Kārttikeya, the divine warrior who slays Tāraka. The boon, granted by Śiva himself, is not merely a reward but a cosmic necessity, aligning individual desire with the universe's order. Kālidāsa's language, rich with *rasa* (aesthetic emotion), elevates these boons into moments of sublime beauty, as when he describes Pārvatī's penance: "Her body, wasted by austerity, glowed like a flame in a windless place" (*tapasā kṣīṇaśarīrā saṃtapati sma nirvāte dīpā iva*).

Aśvaghoṣa, in his *Buddhacaritam*, employs boons to underscore the spiritual quest. The Buddha, before his enlightenment, is offered boons by Māra, the tempter, who promises worldly dominion. Yet, Siddhārtha's rejection of these boons' material wealth and power marks his transcendence, a narrative pivot that contrasts the ephemeral allure of *varas* with the eternal truth of *nirvāṇa*. Aśvaghoṣa's measured verses, steeped in Buddhist philosophy, frame boons as tests of resolve, their rejection a triumph of the spirit.

The Weight of the Curse: *Śāpa* as Karmic Reckoning

If boons elevate, curses ground the narrative in the stark reality of human frailty and divine justice. A *śāpa*, often pronounced by a sage or deity in a moment of righteous anger, serves as a moral corrective, a reminder of *dharma's* inviolable boundaries. Yet, these curses are rarely absolute; they often carry an escape clause, a glimmer of redemption that softens their severity.

Bhāsa, the dramatist of raw emotional power, masterfully employs curses in his plays. In *Ūrubhaṅga*, the tragic tale of Duryodhana's fall, the curse of doom hangs implicitly over the Kuru dynasty, a consequence of their *adharma*. Bhāsa's portrayal of Duryodhana's final moments, where he accepts his fate with stoic dignity, transforms the curse into a meditation on mortality and honour. The playwright's terse yet evocative dialogue "My heart is not broken, though my thighs are" (*na me hṛdayaṃ bhinnaṃ yadyapi bhinnau me sakthīnī*) captures the human spirit's resilience under the weight of divine retribution.

Bhāravi's *Kirātārjunīyam* presents a nuanced interplay of boon and curse. Arjuna's quest for divine weapons from Śiva, disguised as a *Kirāta*, is framed by the boon of Pāśupata, a weapon of cosmic potency. Yet, the narrative hints at the curse of hubris that shadows Arjuna's ambition, as his pride in his archery skills is tested by Śiva's challenge. Bhāravi's intricate *alaṅkāras* (poetic ornaments) weave a tapestry of tension, where the boon's attainment is fraught with trials, reflecting the delicate balance between divine favour and human striving.

Māgha, in his *Śiśupālavadham*, explores curses as catalysts of cosmic conflict. The antagonist Śiśupāla, cursed by the sage Śrīdāman to be slain by Kṛṣṇa after a hundred insults, embodies the inevitability of fate. Māgha's opulent verses, dense with *śabda-alaṅkāra* (sound-based ornaments), amplify the curse's gravity, as Śiśupāla's taunts crescendo toward his doomed end. The curse, here, is not merely punitive but a narrative fulcrum, orchestrating the triumph of *dharma* over defiance.

Śrīharṣa's *Naiṣadhīyacarita*, a tour de force of erudition, presents the curse as a complex interplay of love and fate. Nala, cursed by Kali to lose his kingdom and endure separation from Damayantī, navigates a labyrinth of suffering. Yet, Śrīharṣa's ornate style transforms this *śāpa* into a poetic exploration of endurance and redemption, with Damayantī's unwavering love serving as the boon that counters the curse. The poet's description of their reunion "Like a lotus blooming under the moon's caress" (*candrikāsparśena kamalaṃ iva*) bathes the narrative in luminous hope.

The Duality of *Vara* and *Śāpa*: A Cosmic Dance

The interplay of boons and curses in Sanskrit literature reflects a deeper philosophical truth: the duality of existence, where joy and sorrow, fortune and misfortune, are inseparable. This duality is poignantly captured in Kālidāsa's *Meghadūtam*, where the Yakṣa's curse of exile for neglecting his duties is tempered by the boon of hope, as he sends a cloud-messenger to his beloved. The poet's imagery "The cloud, heavy with rain, moves like my heart, heavy with longing" (*megho meghavān iva me hṛdayaṃ kāmāśayena saṃnādati*) blends sorrow and beauty, curse and aspiration, into a singular aesthetic experience.

In Aśvaghoṣa's *Saundarānanda*, the curse of worldly attachment binds Nanda to *saṃsāra*, yet the boon of the

Buddha's teachings offers liberation. The poet's serene verses contrast the transient boons of sensual pleasure with the eternal vara of enlightenment, inviting readers to transcend the cycle of curses and rewards.

Bhāsa's *Svapnavāsavadattm* further illustrates this duality. The curse of misunderstanding separates King Udayana from Vāsavadattā, but the boon of divine intervention, disguised as a dream, restores their bond. Bhāsa's deft handling of *rasa śṛṅgāra* (romance) tempered by *vīra* (heroism) makes the resolution a triumph of love over fate.

The Aesthetic and Moral Resonance

Boons and curses in Sanskrit literature are not mere narrative tools but bearers of profound aesthetic and moral weight. The *rasa* evoked by a *vara* whether the *śānta* (peace) of spiritual triumph or the *śṛṅgāra* of love fulfilled elevates the reader's soul. Conversely, the *śāpa*, with its *karuṇa* (pathos) or *raudra* (wrath), grounds the narrative in the human struggle against fate. The poets' mastery lies in balancing these forces, creating a symphony of emotions that resonates across centuries.

Kālidāsa's lyrical finesse, Bhāsa's dramatic intensity, Aśvaghoṣa's spiritual depth, Bhāravi's intellectual rigor, Māgha's verbal opulence, and Śrīharṣa's philosophical complexity converge in their portrayal of boons and curses as mirrors of the human condition. These literary gems, studded with *alaṅkāras* and imbued with *dharma*, invite us to ponder the delicate balance of free will and destiny, the transient nature of boons, and the redemptive potential of curses.

In the end, Sanskrit classical literature teaches us that

boons and curses are two sides of the same cosmic coin, each shaping the other in the eternal dance of creation and dissolution. As Kālidāsa writes in *Raghuvaṃśam*, "The wheel of fate turns, now lifting, now casting down" (*cakram īśvarasya saṃparivartati uccairnīcaiśca*). In this turning, the stories of gods and mortals, blessings and burdens, continue to enchant and enlighten, their echoes resounding in the heart of Indian mythology.

❑

Chapter VIII

The Subtle Mystery of Curses and Boons in Mythology

Divya-śakti, Pātratā, and the Cosmic Law

In the deep philosophical labyrinthine intricacies of Indian mythology, the phenomena of *vara* (boon) and *śāpa* (curse) operate not merely as narrative devices but as profound metaphysical principles governing the destinies of gods, sages, kings, and ordinary beings alike. The *Purāṇas*, those ageless chronicles of cosmic events, brim with narratives wherein mortal lives have been uplifted and transformed by the grace of a boon, or conversely, cast into misfortune by the sting of a curse. These are not arbitrary occurrences but outcomes dictated by the subtleties of merit (*pātratā*), intent, and the immutable laws of *ṛta* the cosmic order.

The Sanctity of Boons (*Varadāna*) and the Law of Deservedness

It is a well-acknowledged truth in the ancient Indian worldview that *divyātmā* enlightened souls bestow their grace only upon those who possess the requisite eligibility. As the aphorism goes:

"pātratāṁ vina dātuṁ na śakyate varaḥ"

(Without worthiness, a boon cannot be conferred.)

The *Purāṇas* recount countless episodes where kings, ascetics, householders, or even the downtrodden have attained impossible triumphs through divine favour, blessings born of inner purity, relentless *tapas* (penance), and moral steadfastness. However, these boons are never frivolously granted. Just as the earth yields grain only to the one who tills it, and the cow offers milk only when milked with care, so too do the divine forces respond to true effort, sacrifice, and virtue.

Not mere vocal pleas, gestures of flattery, or superficial offerings can elicit such gifts. Only profound inner emotion, marked by purity of intent and unyielding perseverance, can touch the heart of the divine. A guru's blessing, a mother's prayer, or a sage's glance when genuinely earned can uplift a soul from the abyss of despair to the zenith of fortune.

Boons: The Currency of *Tapas* and *Tyāga*

It must be understood that *tapas* is not the mere affliction of the body but a profound commitment to ideals, a readiness to sacrifice for the good, and the courage to endure hardship for higher principles. The *divyātmā* dispenses their *tapas-sampatti* the wealth of their spiritual merit only after discerning the recipient's worthiness, sincerity, and the potential consequences of their boon. An ancient adage asserts:

"dānād api varaḥ pradhānaḥ"

(A boon is nobler than a mere gift.)

While a material donation perishes, a boon alters fate itself, casting a new step into the land of destiny. Yet, even this sacred act is bound by ethical discernment. The *divyātmā* must contemplate: Who deserves this? To what purpose? What consequences shall arise?

The *Purāṇas* illustrate this principle through myriad narratives. Śrī Rāvaṇa, having pleased Lord Śaṅkara with austerities, received boons that made him nearly invincible, yet his unrestrained ambition brought his ruin. Conversely, *Bhakta* Śabarī's humble devotion earned her the grace of Śrī Rāma. Thus, while boons are potent, their bestowal is neither random nor indulgent.

Curses (*Śāpa*): The Fiery Fruit of Wrath

As effective as the blessings of the wise are, equally terrifying is their wrath, manifesting as *śāpa*. When a person of immense *ātma-bala* (spiritual might) is deeply wronged, the consequence is not merely emotional, but cosmic. A *śāpa*, issued with righteous indignation, becomes an unalterable law of fate.

Ancient texts are replete with accounts where individuals, violating dharma or causing anguish to the virtuous, were consigned to dreadful fates. The *Purāṇas* remind us:

"aparādhān mahānṛṇāṁ śāpaḥ pātyati duṣkṛtam"

(The curse of the great falls heavily upon the wicked.)

The destruction of King Sagara's sons by Kapila Muni, the snakebite death of Parīkṣit due to Śṛṅgi's curse, and the annihilation of the Yādava clan as a result of Gāndhārī's grief-fuelled malediction are legendary illustrations of this principle.

Even material objects, lands, and relics have borne the imprint of curses. The ominous fate of the Hope Diamond and the tragic history of cursed artifacts across cultures reveal a consistent theme: when divine order is violated, repercussions ensue.

Curses in the Modern Context: The Continuance of Ancient Patterns

Even in contemporary times, such phenomena have not been relegated to mere myth. Stories of lands refusing habitation, artifacts bringing ruin, or individuals falling prey to inexplicable tragedies persist. The account of Tutankhamun's tomb, the misfortunes trailing the Hope Diamond, and cursed estates like those in Karachi reinforce the ancient belief that cosmic justice is inescapable.

While rationality dismisses these as coincidences or superstition, deeper inquiry often reveals patterns too precise to ignore. The law of causation (*kārya-kāraṇa-bhāva*) in Indian philosophy holds that every effect must have a cause, visible or subtle. Thus, curses, when viewed through this lens, are not irrational superstitions but metaphysical mechanisms to restore balance.

The Moral Foundation of Boons and Curses

Crucially, Indian wisdom maintains that neither boons nor curses arise unprovoked. A true *śāpa* emerges not from petulance but righteous indignation, and a *vara* flows not from indulgence but compassionate discernment. The case of Sage Durvāsā cursing Ambarīṣa, which rebounded upon himself due to the king's innocence, exemplifies that the misuse of such power leads to self-destruction.

This doctrine upholds a central tenet: *adharma* invariably attracts suffering, whether through natural consequences, societal retribution, or divine wrath. Those aligned with dharma need fear neither curse nor calamity.

"na dharmavān vinaśyati"

The righteous never perish.

Conclusion

The traditions of *vara* and *śāpa* are profound affirmations of the moral fabric underpinning existence. They emphasize that divine grace and righteous indignation are not arbitrary but deeply entwined with human conduct, intention, and merit.

As contemporary seekers, our task is not to dismiss these as relics of an archaic past, but to understand their symbolic, ethical, and metaphysical import. In the orchestration of cosmic law, these forces remind us that while fate may be mysterious, it is never unjust.

"*yad bhāvyam tad bhaviṣyati*" what is destined by the law of righteousness shall inevitably come to pass.

And within this eternal dance of cause and consequence, the phenomena of curses and boons continue to weave the intricate patterns of human destiny, in myth and in life.

❑

Chapter IX

The Role of Curses and Boons in Purāṇic Mythology

In the broad spectrum of Purāṇic mythology, where the divine and mortal dance in tune with an eternal interplay of fate and will, curses (*śāpa*) and boons (*vara*) result their cosmic consequences of unpredictable nature. These twin forces, bestowed by sages, gods, or celestial beings, are not mere whims of divine caprice but pivotal instruments that shape the destinies of gods, demons, sages, and mortals alike. They ripple through the vast ocean of existence, altering the course of cosmological events, sparking transformations, and birthing legends that echo through the ages. In the *Purāṇas*, these sacred narratives pulse with the rhythm of *ṛta* the cosmic order where curses and boons serve as divine catalysts, balancing dharma and adharma, creation and destruction, suffering and salvation.

Cosmological Events Shaped by Curses and Boons

The *Purāṇas*, repositories of timeless wisdom, depict a universe where the interplay of curses and boons orchestrates grand cosmological spectacles. These acts of divine will are not mere interventions but the very scaffolding upon which the cosmos unfolds. Consider the epochal *Samudra*

Manthana, the churning of the ocean, a celestial endeavor born of a curse and propelled by a boon. When the sage Durvāsas, fiery in temperament, cursed the gods to lose their immortality for slighting his garland, the *devas* faced a dire calamity. Stripped of their divine vigour, they sought refuge in Lord Viṣṇu, who granted them a boon: the promise of *amṛta*, the nectar of immortality, hidden in the depths of the cosmic ocean. Thus began the great churning, where gods and demons, united by necessity, churned the Kṣīra Sāgara with Mount Mandara as the pivot and Vāsuki, the serpent king, as the rope. From this tumult emerged treasures divine Lakṣmī, the goddess of prosperity, the celestial horse Uccaiḥśravas, and the lethal poison *hālāhala*, which Śiva, in his boundless compassion, consumed to save creation. The curse of Durvāsas, though born of wrath, set in motion a cosmic event that restored balance, while Viṣṇu's boon ensured the triumph of *dharma*.

Curses and boons, in their dual nature, often serve as the fulcrum of cosmic equilibrium. They are the breath of *ṛta*, ensuring that no act, virtuous or vile, escapes the scales of justice. In the *Purāṇas*, they are the divine pen strokes that rewrite destinies, sculpting the very architecture of the universe.

Transformation of Gods, Demons, Sages, and Mortals

The transformative power of curses and boons is a recurring motif in Purāṇic lore, where beings divine and mortal undergo profound metamorphoses. A curse, though cloaked in suffering, often becomes a pathway to redemption, while a boon, radiant with promise, may lead to unforeseen trials. The *Purāṇas* are abound with tales of such transformations, where the divine word reshapes existence itself.

Take the tale of Jaya and Vijaya, the gatekeepers of Viṣṇu's celestial abode, Vaikuṇṭha. When the Kumāras, four sage-like sons of Brahmā, sought entry to meet the Lord, Jaya and Vijaya, in their zealous guardianship, barred their path, mistaking their divine intent. Enraged by this affront, the Kumāras pronounced a curse: the gatekeepers would fall from their divine station to be born as mortals in the earthly realm. Yet, in their mercy, the sages tempered the curse with a choice seven lives as devotees of Viṣṇu or three as his adversaries. Jaya and Vijaya chose the latter, and thus began their cyclical incarnations as Hiraṇyākṣa and Hiraṇyakaśipu, Rāvaṇa and Kumbhakarṇa, and Śiśupāla and Dantavakra. Each life, marked by enmity with Viṣṇu's *avatāras*, was a step toward their ultimate liberation, for even in their antagonism, they were bound to the divine. The curse, though severe, was a crucible for their salvation, illustrating the Purāṇic truth that suffering, when woven with divine intent, becomes a ladder to *mokṣa*.

Mortals, too, are reshaped by these forces. The Pāṇḍavas, central figures of the *Mahābhārata*, owe their births to boons granted to Kuntī and Mādrī by the sage Durvāsas. His *mantra*, a divine gift, allowed Kuntī to summon gods to beget her sons Yudhiṣṭhira from Dharma, Bhīma from Vāyu, Arjuna from Indra, and Nakula and Sahadeva from the Aśvins. These boons transformed a childless lineage into the cornerstone of dharma's triumph, yet they also tethered the Pāṇḍavas to trials ordained by fate. Similarly, the birth of Skanda, the war-god, was the fruit of Śiva's boon to the devas, who sought a commander to vanquish the demon Tāraka. Born from Śiva's divine spark, Skanda's emergence was a testament to the boon's power to birth divine warriors. Likewise, Gaṇeśa, the remover of obstacles, came into being through Pārvatī's fervent desire, blessed by Śiva's acquiescence, embodying the transformative grace of a boon.

Demons, too, are not spared the alchemy of curses and boons. The demon Tāraka, granted a boon by Brahmā that only Śiva's son could slay him, revelled in his invincibility until Skanda's birth fulfilled the prophecy. The boon, a shield of temporary triumph, ultimately paved the way for his downfall, underscoring the Purāṇic paradox that even the mightiest gifts carry the seeds of their own reversal.

Famous Episodes

The Churning of the Ocean (*Samudra Manthana*)

The *Samudra Manthana* stands as a luminous testament to the interplay of curse and boon. Durvāsas' curse upon the *devas*, stripping them of their divine splendor, was the spark that ignited this cosmic endeavor. Viṣṇu's boon, guiding them to churn the ocean for *amṛta*, transformed despair into a saga of creation. The collaboration of *devas* and asuras, fraught with tension, birthed wonders Dhanvantarī with the nectar, the celestial elephant Airāvata, and the wish-fulfilling tree Kalpavṛkṣa. Yet, the emergence of *hālāhala* tested Śiva's compassion, as he swallowed the poison to preserve the cosmos, earning the epithet Nīlakaṇṭha, the blue-throated one. This episode encapsulates the Purāṇic vision of curses as catalysts for creation and boons as beacons of hope, harmonizing the forces of chaos and order.

The Story of Jaya and Vijaya

The tale of Jaya and Vijaya is a poignant narrative of fall and redemption. Their curse, born of a momentary lapse, cast them into the mortal coil, yet it was a divine orchestration. As Hiraṇyākṣa and Hiraṇyakaśipu, they challenged Viṣṇu's *avatāras*, Varāha and Narasiṃha; as Rāvaṇa and Kumbhakarṇa, they stood against Rāma; as Śiśupāla and Dantavakra, they faced Kṛṣṇa. Each life, though steeped in *adharma*, was a step toward their return to Vaikuṇṭha. The curse, a seeming punishment, was a divine boon in disguise, for it bound them to Viṣṇu's eternal presence, proving that even the darkest decrees serve the light of liberation.

The Births of the Pāṇḍavas, Skanda, and Gaṇeśa

The births of the Pāṇḍavas, Skanda, and Gaṇeśa illuminate the transformative power of boons. Kuntī's boon from Durvāsas birthed heroes destined to uphold dharma, their divine lineage shaping the *Mahābhārata's* epic struggle. Skanda, born of Śiva's boon to the devas, emerged as the spear-wielding Karttikeya, slayer of Tāraka, his birth a triumph of divine will over demonic hubris. Gaṇeśa, born of Pārvatī's longing and Śiva's grace, became the beloved *Vighnahartā*, remover of obstacles, his elephantine form a symbol of wisdom and auspiciousness. These births, sparked by boons, anticipate a timeless horizon where divine gifts birth legends that guide humanity toward *dharma*.

Conclusion

In the *Purāṇas*, curses and boons are the warp and weft of a cosmic loom, crafting narratives that resonate with eternal truths. They are not mere tools of reward or retribution but divine instruments that sculpt the destinies of gods, demons, and mortals. From the churning of the ocean to the births of divine heroes, these forces shape the cosmos, reminding us that every curse carries the seed of redemption, and every boon bears the weight of responsibility. In their dance, we glimpse the eternal rhythm of *ṛta*, where suffering and salvation, chaos and creation, are but two sides of the same divine truth.

❑

Chapter X

The Mechanism and Ethics of Curses and Boons in Purāṇic Mythology

In the profuse richness of Indian mythology, where the threads of fate weave destinies across the cosmic loom, curses (*śāpa*) and boons (*vara*) emerge as divine instruments of transformation. These are not mere utterances of wrath or benevolence but sacred decrees that result through the workings of existence, binding the mortal and divine to the eternal rhythm of *ṛta* the cosmic order. In the *Purāṇas*, curses and boons are the breath of destiny, shaping lives, altering realms, and upholding the delicate balance of *dharma*. Yet, their invocation raises profound questions: Who wields such power? What conditions govern their pronouncement? And how do they interplay with the immutable doctrine of *karma*? This chapter delves into the mechanisms, ethics, and cosmic implications of these divine acts, unveiling their role as both arbiters of justice and catalysts of moral inquiry.

Who Can Give a Curse or Boon and Why

In the Purāṇic cosmos, the authority to bestow curses or boons is not granted lightly; it is a privilege reserved for beings of extraordinary spiritual potency. Sages (*ṛṣis*), steeped in the fire of *tapas* (austerity), wield this power through their accumulated merit. Their words, infused with the energy of penance, can alter destinies, as seen when Durvāsas cursed the *devas* for slighting his garland, plunging them into mortality. Gods, as embodiments of cosmic principles, also possess this authority. Brahmā, Viṣṇu, and Śiva frequently grant boons to devotees or demons, often to fulfill divine purposes or test mortal virtue. Even celestial beings, such as gandharvas or apsaras, may pronounce curses when affronted, though their power is lesser, tempered by their divine station.

The reasons for bestowing curses or boons are as varied as the stars in the firmament. Curses often arise from righteous indignation, as when a sage's honour is violated or *dharma* is transgressed. The curse of Gautama upon Ahalyā, transforming her to stone for her indiscretion, was not mere punishment but a corrective measure to restore moral order. Boons, conversely, are often rewards for devotion, penance, or valour. When Arjuna performed severe austerities to please Śiva, the boon of the Pāśupata weapon elevated him to a warrior of cosmic significance. Yet, boons granted to demons, such as Rāvaṇa's near-invincibility from Brahmā, reveal a deeper purpose: they test the resilience of *dharma*, setting the stage for divine intervention through *avatāras*. Thus, curses and boons are not arbitrary but purposeful, aligning with the cosmic dance of creation, preservation, and destruction.

Conditions, Triggers, and Consequences

The pronouncement of a curse or boon is governed by intricate conditions and triggers, ensuring they serve the greater good of *ṛta*. A curse, though born of wrath, is rarely absolute; it often carries a condition for its reversal, a glimmer of mercy woven into its severity. When the sage Viśvāmitra cursed Triśaṅku to become a *chaṇḍāla* for his hubris, he tempered the curse with the promise of a celestial abode, albeit an imperfect one. Similarly, boons are not boundless; they come with stipulations that reflect the recipient's intent or the granter's foresight. Tāraka's boon of invincibility, granted by Brahmā, was conditioned on his death by Śiva's son, ensuring the demon's tyranny would not endure unchecked.

Triggers for curses often stem from violations of *dharma* disrespect to a sage, betrayal, or hubris. Boons, however, are triggered by acts of devotion, sacrifice, or penance, as when Kuntī received Durvāsas' mantra for her selfless service. The consequences of these acts are profound, rippling across lifetimes and realms. A curse may plunge a soul into suffering, as with Jaya and Vijaya, who fell from Vaikuṇṭha to mortal births, yet it also paves the path to liberation. A boon, while granting power or prosperity, may sow the seeds of downfall if misused, as seen in Hiraṇyakaśipu's boon, which led to his confrontation with Narasiṃha. Thus, curses and boons are not ends but beginnings, initiating cycles of action and consequence that resonate with the cosmic order.

Ethical Dilemmas and Cosmic Balance

The invocation of curses and boons raises intricate ethical dilemmas, challenging the boundaries of justice and compassion. Is a sage's curse, born of momentary anger, justified when it dooms a soul to lifetimes of suffering? Does a boon granted to a demon, knowing it may unleash chaos, align with *dharma*? These questions lie at the heart of Purāṇic narratives, where the interplay of free will and divine will creates a moral maping of breathtaking complexity.

Consider the curse of Gāndhārī upon Kṛṣṇa, blaming him for the Kurukṣetra war's devastation. Her anguish was righteous, yet her curse that Kṛṣṇa's Yādava clan would perish tested the ethics of retribution against a divine avatāra. Kṛṣṇa, in his infinite wisdom, accepted the curse, for it aligned with the cosmic necessity of his earthly departure. Similarly, boons granted to demons like Rāvaṇa or Tāraka pose a dilemma: they empower adharma, yet their very granting ensures its eventual defeat, as divine *avatāras* rise to restore balance. This paradox clarifies the Purāṇic view that curses and boons, while seemingly disruptive, are instruments of cosmic equilibrium, ensuring that no act escapes the scales of justice.

The ethical tension is further heightened when boons are misused. A boon, intended as a reward, may become a curse when wielded with pride or malice. Bhasmāsura, granted the power to reduce anyone to ashes by touch, turned his boon against Śiva himself, only to be outwitted by Viṣṇu's Mohinī form. Here, the ethical dilemma lies in the granter's foresight: did Śiva not anticipate the demon's treachery? The *Purāṇas* suggest that such boons are deliberate, serving as tests of character or catalysts for divine intervention, preserving the cosmic balance between *dharma* and *adharma*.

Doctrine of *Karma* and Its Interplay

At the heart of curses and boons lies the doctrine of karma, the immutable law of cause and effect that governs all existence. Curses and boons are not exceptions to *karma* but its instruments, channeling its flow through divine or sagely will. A curse is often the fruition of past *karma*, a consequence of actions that demand redress. When Ahalyā was cursed by Gautama, it was not merely for her transgression but a reflection of karmic debt, mitigated by the promise of liberation through Rāma's touch. Similarly, boons are rewards for virtuous *karma*, as when Arjuna's penance earned him Śiva's favour.

Yet, the interplay of curses, boons, and *karma* is not linear. A boon may delay the consequences of *karma*, as with Rāvaṇa, whose invincibility postponed his reckoning until Rāma's arrow struck. A curse may accelerate karmic retribution, as with Jaya and Vijaya, whose fall hastened their path to *mokṣa*. The *Purāṇas* teach that these divine acts are woven into the karmic fabric, ensuring that every soul, whether god, demon, or mortal, navigates the cycle of action and consequence toward ultimate liberation.

This interplay also reveals the fluidity of karma. A curse, though a punishment, may purify the soul, cleansing past misdeeds. A boon, while a reward, may entangle the recipient in new karmic bonds if misused. The sage Nārada's curse upon the sons of Kubera, turning them into trees, was a lesson in humility, their liberation by Kṛṣṇa a testament to *karma's* redemptive arc. Thus, curses and boons are not mere divine whims but sacred mechanisms that align individual destinies with the cosmic dance of karma and *ṛta*.

Conclusion

In the vast annals of Purāṇic mythology, curses and boons are the divine brushstrokes that paint the canvas of existence. Wielded by sages, gods, and celestial beings, they are not arbitrary but purposeful, governed by conditions that reflect the cosmic order. Their ethical dilemmas balancing justice with compassion, power with responsibility reveal the profound complexity of dharma. Intertwined with the doctrine of *karma*, they serve as catalysts of transformation, guiding souls through cycles of suffering and salvation. In their interplay, we glimpse the eternal truth of the *Purāṇas*: that every curse holds the promise of redemption, and every boon carries the weight of destiny, forever bound to the rhythm of *ṛta*.

❑

Chapter XI

The Interference of Fate: Curses and Boons in Epic Narratives

In the vast realm of Indian mythology, where the eternal pulse of *ṛta* weaves destinies across the cosmic loom, curses (*śāpa*) and boons (*vara*) shimmer as divine utterances that shape the fates of gods, mortals, and demons alike. These sacred pronouncements, whether born of wrath or grace, are not mere words but potent forces that ripple through the ages, binding the epic narratives of the *Rāmāyaṇa* and *Mahābhārata* to the timeless dance of *dharma* and *karma*. From the anguished curse of Tārā upon Rāma to the redemptive boons granted to Draupadī, these decrees illuminate the interplay of human frailty and divine will. This chapter delves into a rich catalogue of both celebrated and lesser-known *śāpa* and *vara*, revealing their profound impact on the heroes, sages, and deities who define India's mythological legacy.

The Cosmic Weight of Curses

Curses in Indian mythology are not mere outbursts of anger but sacred instruments of justice, tempering hubris and restoring balance to the cosmic order. They are the voice of *ṛta*, ensuring that no transgression escapes the scales of *dharma*. Among the most poignant is Tārā's *śāpa* upon Rāma, pronounced in the wake of Vāli's death during his duel with Sugrīva. In her grief, Tārā cursed Rāma that he would lose Sītā soon after regaining her, and that Sītā would return to the earth. She further declared that in his next birth, as Śrī Kṛṣṇa, Rāma would be slain by Vāli, reborn as a hunter. This *śāpa*, woven into the *Rāmāyaṇa*, underscores the ripple of consequences, where even a divine *avatāra* bears the weight of mortal actions.

Equally defining is the curse of the Sanatkumāras upon Jaya and Vijaya, Viṣṇu's gatekeepers, whose refusal to admit the sages to Vaikuṇṭha sparked a *śāpa* that cast them into mortal realms as Hiraṇyākṣa, Hiraṇyakaśipu, Rāvaṇa, and Kumbhakarṇa. This curse, a cornerstone of Purāṇic lore, necessitated Viṣṇu's four *avatāras* to liberate them, illustrating the redemptive arc woven into even the harshest decrees. Similarly, the curse upon King Daśaratha by Śravaṇa Kumāra's parents, grieving their son's accidental death, foretold his suffering through separation from Rāma, a consequence amplified by Kaikeyī's boons. These *śāpa* reveal the intricate interplay of fate, where suffering becomes a crucible for spiritual evolution.

The tale of Ahalyā, cursed by Sage Gautama to become stone for her unwitting liaison with Indra, is a haunting narrative of punishment and redemption. Liberated by Rāma's touch, her *śāpa* symbolizes the silencing of agency, yet her *vara*-like restoration reflects the mercy inherent in divine justice. Gautama's curse upon Indra, transforming him into *Sahasrayoni* (thousand female genitals) before granting the boon of *Sahasrākṣa* (thousand eyes), further illustrates the transformative duality of *śāpa* and *vara*, where retribution paves the way for renewal.

Karna, the tragic hero of the *Mahābhārata*, bears a litany of curses that underscore his doomed valour. Paraśurāma's *śāpa* ensured Karna would forget his *mantra* at the moment of greatest need, while Bhūmi Devī cursed his chariot wheel to sink in battle, and a brahmin's curse foretold his helpless death for killing a cow. These curses, compounding his fate, highlight the relentless grip of *karma*. Yet, Karna's boon to Kuntī, promising to spare her sons save Arjuna, reveals his nobility, a *vara* that softens the shadow of his cursed existence.

The Radiance of Boons

Boons, as radiant counterparts to curses, are divine gifts that elevate, empower, or redeem, yet often carry the seeds of their own trials. Kuntī's vara from Durvāsas, granting her the mantra to summon gods, birthed the Pāṇḍavas, weaving her agency into the tapestry of *dharma*. This boon, born of her selfless service, transformed a childless widow into the mother of heroes, yet tethered her to the trials of the *Mahābhārata*. Similarly, Draupadī's boons from Śiva, granting her five husbands and perpetual virginity, reshaped her destiny as the Pāṇḍavas' wife, a vara that balanced her desires with the burden of navigating a polyandrous union within a patriarchal world.

Meghnād's boon from Brahmā, rendering him invincible until his Nikumbalā *yajña* was disrupted, empowered his martial prowess but set the stage for Lakṣmaṇa's triumph. Jayadratha's father, Vṛddhakṣatra, granted a chilling *vara* that anyone causing his son's head to fall to the ground would suffer their own head bursting into a thousand pieces, a boon outwitted by Arjuna's strategic archery. Bhīṣma's boon from Śāntanu, allowing him to choose his time of death, elevated his vow of celibacy but bound him to the tragic sidelines of the *Mahābhārata* war. These *vara* illuminate the paradox of divine gifts: they uplift, yet demand wisdom to wield.

Hanumān, the devoted vanara, received boons from Brahmā and Sūrya, rendering him immune to weapons and capable of altering his form with *laghimā* and *garimā*. These gifts, pivotal in the *Sundarā Kāṇḍa*, enabled his heroic feats, yet his childhood curse from sages forgetting his powers until reminded underscored the humility required to harness such boons. Similarly, Anjanā, Hanumān's mother, transformed from an apsara to a vanara by a sage's curse, was redeemed by Brahmā's *vara*, promising liberation through birthing Śiva's incarnation. These narratives reveal boons as pathways to transcendence, often intertwined with the trials of curses.

The Interplay of *Śāpa* and *Vara*

The dance of *śāpa* and *vara* in Indian mythology is a symphony of balance, where retribution and grace converge to uphold *ṛta*. Gāndhārī's curse upon Śrī Kṛṣṇa, blaming him for the *Mahābhārata* war, foretold the Yādava clan's destruction, a śāpa accepted by Kṛṣṇa as part of his divine leela. Yet, Kṛṣṇa himself wielded curses, as with Samba, afflicted with leprosy, and Aśvatthāmā, condemned to eternal life for his heinous act against Pārikṣit. These acts reflect the divine interplay of justice and mercy, where curses serve as karmic reckonings and boons as redemptive promises.

The curse of Nārada upon Viṣṇu, rendering him dependent on *vānaras*, was fulfilled through Hanumān's devotion in the *Rāmāyaṇa*, while Nārada's *śāpa* upon Kubera's sons, Nalakūvara and Maṇigrīva, transformed them into trees until liberated by Kṛṣṇa. These cycles of curse and liberation project the Purāṇic vision of *karma*, where suffering is a crucible for spiritual ascent. Similarly, Śiva's boons to Arjuna (the Pāśupata *astra*) and Gaṇeśa (primacy in worship) elevate their roles, while his curse upon Brahmā, barring his worship, reflects the divine recalibration of ego. Sarasvatī's complementary curse upon Brahmā and her own transformation into a tree through mutual curses with Lakṣmī and Gaṅgā weave a complex web of divine reciprocity, highlighting the interconnectedness of all beings.

The Eternal Echoes of the Spoken Word

The *śāpa* and *vara* of Indian mythology are not mere relics of ancient tales but living echoes of the spoken word's sanctity. They remind us that words, whether uttered in wrath or benevolence, carry the weight of creation and destruction. The curse of Rādhā upon Śrīdhāmā, separating her from Kṛṣṇa, and Śrīdhāmā's reciprocal *śāpa*, reflect the human emotions of love and betrayal, while Śiva's boon to Draupadī ensures her sanctity across her marriages. The curse upon Śāntanu and Gaṅgā by Brahmā, casting them as mortals, and the liberation of Kabandha by Rāma, freed from a rākṣasa's form, weave narratives of fall and redemption, where śāpa and vara serve as twin pillars of *dharma*.

These stories, from the tragic curses upon Karna to the triumphant boons of Hanumān, resonate with the eternal truth of Indian thought: that every word shapes destiny, every act ripples through karma. They teach humility, as seen in Hanumān's forgotten powers; resilience, as in Ahalyā's redemption; and responsibility, as in Draupadī's boons. In their inscrutable interplay, śāpa and vara are not mere divine decrees but mirrors of the soul, reflecting the delicate balance of justice and grace that guides the universe toward *mokṣa*.

Conclusion

Thus Indian mythology replete with curses and boons are the breath of *ṛta*, sculpting the destinies of gods, mortals, and demons with the power of the spoken word. From Tārā's anguished *śāpa* upon Rāma to Kuntī's transformative *vara*, these decrees weave a canvass of trial and triumph, retribution and redemption. They are the heartbeat of the *Rāmāyaṇa* and *Mahābhārata*, pulsing through the lives of Karna, Gaṇeśa, and Hiraṇyakaśipu, reminding us that no act escapes the cosmic ledger of *karma*. As we trace their echoes from the fiery curses of sages to the radiant boons of gods we glimpse the eternal dance of *dharma*, where every word, every intention, shapes the soul's journey toward the divine. In this divine interplay, the spoken word endures as a sacred force, its power to curse and bless forever binding us to the timeless rhythm of the cosmos.

❑

Chapter XII

Symbolism and Psychological Interpretations of Curses and Boons

In Indian mythology, where the divine and human are in a confluence of eternal truths, curses (*śāpa*) and boons (*vara*) are not mere narrative devices but radiant symbols that illuminate the human condition. Within the *Purāṇas*, these sacred pronouncements transcend their immediate context, becoming mirrors of the psyche and emblems of cosmic wisdom. They speak to the deepest recesses of the soul, weaving tales of reward and retribution, desire and fear that resonate across time. This chapter explores the symbolic meanings of curses and boons, their embodiment of psychological archetypes, and the profound lessons they impart for human behaviour and morality, inviting us to gaze into the eternal mirror of *ṛta* the cosmic order and find our own reflections.

Symbolic Meanings of Curses and Boons in Myths

Curses and boons in Purāṇic mythology are the basic modus operandi for existence, each carrying a symbolic weight that transcends the literal. A curse, though cloaked in suffering, is a symbol of disruption an unraveling of harmony that demands restoration. It represents the inevitable consequence of transgressing *dharma*, the moral law that binds the cosmos. When Gautama cursed Ahalyā to become stone for her indiscretion, the transformation was not merely punitive but symbolic of stagnation a soul frozen in time until redeemed by divine grace, embodied in Rāma's touch. The curse thus becomes a metaphor for the human struggle with guilt, isolation, and the longing for redemption.

Boons, conversely, are radiant symbols of aspiration and divine favour. They embody the fulfillment of desire, the reward for devotion, or the promise of transcendence. When Śiva granted Arjuna the Pāśupata weapon after his arduous penance, the boon symbolized not just martial prowess but the triumph of discipline over chaos, the alignment of human will with divine purpose. Yet, boons also carry a shadow, symbolizing the burden of power and the peril of hubris. Rāvaṇa's boon of near-invincibility from Brahmā, while a mark of his ascetic might, became a symbol of unchecked ambition, leading to his downfall at Rāma's hands. In this duality, curses and boons mirror the eternal tension between limitation and liberation, grounding the *Purāṇas* in the universal quest for balance.

Together, these divine acts symbolize the interplay of *ṛta* and *adharma*, the cosmic dance where every action ripples through the fabric of existence. They are not mere events but archetypes of transformation, reflecting the eternal cycle of fall and redemption, struggle and transcendence, that defines the human journey.

Psychological Archetypes: Reward, Punishment, Desire, Fear

The *Purāṇas*, in their timeless wisdom, weave curses

and boons as psychological archetypes that resonate with the deepest currents of the human psyche. These archetypes reward, punishment, desire, and fear form the scaffolding of the myths, offering insights into the motivations and conflicts that shape human behaviour.

Reward, embodied in boons, is the archetype of fulfillment, the culmination of human striving. The boon granted to Kuntī by Durvāsas, enabling her to summon gods to beget the Pāṇḍavas, reflects the psychological yearning for creation and legacy. It speaks to the universal desire for recognition, for a gift that elevates one's purpose. Yet, the archetype of reward carries a caveat: the responsibility to wield it wisely. Bhasmāsura's boon, which allowed him to reduce anyone to ashes, became a trap when his desire turned to destruction, illustrating the psychological peril of unchecked ambition.

Punishment, manifest in curses, is the archetype of consequence, the shadow cast by actions that disrupt harmony. The curse of the Kumāras upon Jaya and Vijaya, casting them from Vaikuṇṭha to mortal realms, symbolizes the psyche's confrontation with failure and exile. It reflects the fear of losing one's place of falling from grace, yet also the potential for growth through suffering. The curse, tempered by the promise of liberation, becomes a psychological journey from guilt to redemption, a reminder that punishment, when endured with awareness, can purify the soul.

Desire, the driving force behind many boons, is an archetype of longing that fuels both creation and destruction. The *Purāṇas* depict desire as a double-edged sword: Pārvatī's fervent wish for a son birthed Gaṇeśa, the remover of obstacles, while Hiraṇyakaśipu's desire for immortality led to his boon-fueled tyranny and eventual demise. This archetype reveals the psychological tension between aspiration and restraint, urging the soul to seek with humility lest desire becomes a snare.

Fear, often the undercurrent of curses, is the archetype of vulnerability, the dread of loss or retribution. When Gāndhārī cursed Kṛṣṇa for the fall of her sons, her fear of a world bereft of her lineage found voice in divine wrath. Yet, Kṛṣṇa's acceptance of the curse reflects the transcendence of fear, a psychological surrender to the inevitability of *karma*. This archetype teaches that fear, when confronted, becomes a gateway to wisdom, aligning the soul with the cosmic flow.

These archetypes reward, punishment, desire, and fear are not isolated but interwoven, forming a psychological mosaic that mirrors the human experience. Curses and boons, as their vessels, invite us to explore the depths of our motivations, confronting the light and shadow within.

Lessons for Human Behaviour and Morality

The *Purāṇas*, through the lens of curses and boons, offer timeless lessons for human behaviour and morality, guiding the soul toward *dharma*. These narratives are not mere tales but moral compasses, illuminating the virtues and pitfalls that shape a meaningful life.

The first lesson is the sanctity of humility. Curses often befall those who succumb to hubris, as seen when Triśaṅku, in his ambition to ascend to heaven in his mortal form, was cursed by Viśvāmitra. This teaches that pride, unchecked, invites disruption, urging us to temper ambition with reverence for the cosmic order. Boons, too, demand humility Rāvaṇa's downfall reminds us that divine gifts, when wielded with arrogance, become curses in disguise.

The second lesson is the power of resilience. Curses, though painful, are often pathways to redemption. Ahalyā's transformation into stone was not the end but a pause, her liberation by Rāma a testament to the soul's capacity to endure and transcend. This imparts a moral truth: suffering, when met with patience and faith, becomes a crucible for growth, aligning the individual with *mokṣa*.

The third lesson is the balance of desire and responsibility. Boons, as rewards for devotion or penance, reflect the fulfillment of righteous desire, as when Skanda's birth fulfilled the *devas'* plea for a warrior. Yet, the misuse of boons, as with Bhasmāsura, warns against the perils of unchecked desire. The *Purāṇas* teach that moral behaviour lies in aligning desire with *dharma*, ensuring that our aspirations serve the greater good.

Finally, the interplay of curses and boons underscores the inevitability of *karma*. Every act, virtuous or vile, ripples through the cosmos, and curses and boons are its instruments. The story of Jaya and Vijaya, cursed yet destined for liberation, reveals that even suffering serves a higher purpose, guiding the soul toward its divine origin. This lesson urges us to act with awareness, knowing that our choices shape not only our destiny but the cosmic balance itself.

Conclusion

Thus curses and boons in Purāṇic mythology, are more than divine decrees; they are symbols of the human journey, reflecting the eternal dance of *ṛta* and *karma*. As archetypes of reward, punishment, desire, and fear, they unveil the complexities of the psyche, inviting us to confront our motivations and aspirations. Their lessons of humility, resilience, responsibility, and karmic awareness resonate with timeless wisdom, guiding us toward a life aligned with *dharma*. In the mirror of these myths, we see not only the gods and sages but ourselves, our struggles, and our potential for transcendence. Through curses and boons, the *Purāṇas* whisper an eternal truth: that every trial is a step toward redemption, and every gift a call to rise above the self, into the boundless embrace of the divine.

❑

Chapter XIII

Curses and Boons in Regional and Folk Traditions

In the verdant heartlands and coastal expanses of India, where ancient myths intersect with the rhythms of village life, curses (*śāpa*) and boons (*vara*) act as neurons through the oral traditions of Odisha, Bengal, Tamilnadu, and Maharashtra. Far from the grandiose narratives of the *Purāṇas*, these regional tales, whispered by elders under banyan trees and sung in the glow of temple lamps, have led to the growth of divine justice and human aspiration. Here, curses and boons are not merely cosmic decrees but intimate threads in the fabric of community lore, binding mortals to regional deities and village spirits. Rooted in the soil of local traditions, these stories reflect the dreams, fears, and moral compass of the people, shimmering with the eternal dance of *ṛta* the cosmic order.

Odisha: The Hermit's Curse and the Grace of Ākhaṇḍalamaṇi

In the misty groves of Aradi, Odisha, the lore of Lord Ākhaṇḍalamaṇi, a form of Śiva, reverberates with tales of divine retribution and mercy. One such story speaks of King Birabar, a proud ruler who, in a moment of arrogance, disrespected a hermit meditating by the Brāhmaṇī River. Enraged, the hermit pronounced a *śāpa*, transforming the king into a serpent, condemned to slither in the shadows until he atoned through devotion to Ākhaṇḍalamaṇi. Years passed, and the repentant king, now a humble reptile, coiled around the deity's *liṅga*, offering silent prayers. Moved by his penance, Ākhaṇḍalamaṇi granted a *vara*, restoring Birabar's human form and blessing him with wisdom. This tale, preserved in Odia folk narratives, reflects the region's reverence for humility and the transformative power of divine grace.

Bengal: The Curse of Mā Manasā and the Boon of Protection

In the lush deltas of Bengal, the serpent goddess Mā Manasā reigns as a formidable deity, her lore steeped in curses and boons. A popular folktale recounts the merchant Chand Sadagar, who defied Manasā's worship, scorning her serpentine power. Infuriated, Manasā cursed Chand's lineage, unleashing serpents that claimed his sons one by one. Yet, in her dual nature, Manasā offered a vara to Behula, Chand's devoted daughter-in-law, who braved the river's perils to appease the goddess. Through Behula's unwavering devotion, Manasā restored her husband Lakhindar to life, granting the family her eternal protection. This narrative, sung in the Manasā Mangal ballads, underscores Bengal's cultural embrace of surrender to divine will, where curses test resolve and boons reward faith.

Tamil Nadu: The Boon of Murugan and the Curse of Idumban

In Tamil Nadu's rugged hills, the war-god Murugan,

revered as Kārttikeya, is central to tales of divine favour and retribution. A cherished myth tells of Idumban, a demon-turned-devotee, who once challenged Murugan's might. Angered by his hubris, Murugan cursed Idumban to bear two hills as burdens, a *śāpa* that weighed upon his soul. Yet, Idumban's repentance softened the god's heart, and Murugan granted a *vara*, transforming the hills into sacred loads to be carried in devotion during the Thaipusam festival. Idumban became the guardian of Murugan's shrines, his curse a symbol of penance and his boon a testament to redemption. This tale, vibrant in Tamil oral traditions, reflects the region's ethos of discipline and divine mercy.

Maharashtra: The Curse of Khandobā and the Boon of Mhalsa

In the rugged Deccan of Maharashtra, the warrior-god Khandobā, a form of Śiva, is celebrated in folk tales that blend valour with divine justice. One story speaks of a shepherd who, in greed, stole offerings meant for Khandobā's temple. The god, in his wrath, cursed the shepherd to wander as a restless spirit, his wealth turning to ash. But Khandobā's consort, Mhalsa, moved by the shepherd's remorse, interceded with a *vara*, granting him peace as a guardian spirit of Jejuri's sacred hills. This narrative, woven into the Malhari *Māhātmya*, reflects Maharashtra's cultural valourization of repentance and the interplay of divine wrath and compassion in village life.

Role in Regional Deities' Lore

Regional deities, unlike the pan-Indian pantheon, are deeply rooted in local landscapes and communities, their lore shaped by the immediacy of human struggles. Curses and boons in their narratives serve as bridges between the divine and the mortal, reinforcing the deity's authority while offering moral guidance. In Odisha, Ākhaṇḍalamaṇi's curses, like that upon King Birabar, emphasize the sanctity of humility before the divine, while his boons affirm the power of devotion to transcend suffering. In Bengal, Mā Manasā's dual role as a curser and boon-giver reflects her as a guardian of life and death, her *śāpa* purging defiance and her *vara* rewarding surrender. Tamil Nadu's Murugan uses curses to discipline, as with Idumban, and boons to elevate, weaving a narrative of spiritual growth through trial. In Maharashtra, Khandobā's curses punish greed, while his boons, often mediated by Mhalsa, restore balance, reflecting the region's warrior ethos tempered by compassion.

These deities, embedded in local culture, use curses and boons to enforce *dharma* within the community. Their stories, unlike the cosmic scope of Purāṇic tales, are intimate, tied to rivers, hills, and village shrines, making the divine accessible and relatable. The *śāpa* and *vara* become narrative tools to instill reverence, ensuring that the deity's presence is felt in every harvest, festival, and hearth.

Village Myths and Oral Narratives

In the villages of India, where oral traditions breathe life into mythology, curses and boons are the heartbeat of storytelling. These narratives, passed down through generations, are not static but dynamic, shaped by the teller's voice and the listener's heart. In Odisha, elders recount tales of cursed trees and blessed springs, like the story of a banyan in Bhadrak that weeps due to a sage's *śāpa* for sheltering thieves, its tears ceasing only when pilgrims offer prayers to Ākhaṇḍalamaṇi. In Bengal, boatmen sing of Manasā's wrath upon rivers, where a fisherman's curse for neglecting her shrine turned waters treacherous, only calmed by her boon of safe passage.

In Tamil Nadu, village storytellers narrate the tale of a cursed well in Palani, its waters bitter until Murugan's devotees performed rituals to earn his *vara*, restoring its sweetness. In Maharashtra, oral narratives speak of Khandobā's curse upon a barren field, transformed into fertile land after a farmer's penance earned Mhalsa's blessing. These stories, often unrecorded, pulse with the immediacy of local life, tying communities to their deities through shared moral lessons. They teach that curses, though harsh, are calls to atonement, and boons, though radiant, demand responsibility, weaving dharma into the fabric of village existence.

Conclusion

In the vibrant mosaic of India's regional and folk traditions, curses and boons are more than mythological motifs; they are the soul of stories that bind communities to their deities and landscapes. From the serpent-haunted rivers of Bengal to the sacred hills of Tamil Nadu, from Odisha's temple groves to Maharashtra's rugged plateaus, these tales are replete with the interplay of divine wrath and mercy. They reflect upon the human journey through trial and triumph, teaching humility, resilience, and reverence for *dharma*. In the voices of village elders and the chants of festival processions, curses and boons live on, not as distant myths but as living truths, guiding the heart toward the eternal rhythm of *ṛta*.

❑

Chapter XIV

Curses and Boons in Modern Retellings

Indian mythology, in alignment with the eternal dance of *ṛta* for anticipating destinies through divine will, curses (*śāpa*) and boons (*vara*) remain the organic threads of fusion, where their radiance is undimmed by time. In modern India, these ancient motifs find new life in the vibrant realms of literature, cinema, theatre, and television, reimagining the sacred interplay of retribution and grace for contemporary audiences. From the pages of novels to the silver screen, from the intimate stage to the flickering glow of mythological serials, curses and boons persist as potent symbols, resonating with the timeless pulse of *dharma*. This chapter explores how these divine decrees are reinterpreted in modern retellings, their enduring presence in contemporary culture, and the profound influence of Indian television serials in shaping modern perceptions of these cosmic forces.

Literature: Reimagining the Divine Word

In modern Indian literature, curses and boons are rewoven into narratives that blend myth with human complexity, offering fresh perspectives on ancient tales. Authors like Amish Tripathi and Chitra Banerjee Divakaruni breathe new life into these motifs, grounding them in psychological and social contexts. In Tripathi's *Shiva Trilogy*, the boon of immortality granted to characters like Rāvaṇa is reimagined as a burden, a *vara* that fuels ambition but binds the soul to suffering, echoing the Purāṇic paradox of divine gifts. Divakaruni's *The Palace of Illusions*, a retelling of the *Mahābhārata* through Draupadī's eyes, reframes Kuntī's boon from Durvāsas as an act of agency, a woman wielding divine power to shape destiny within a patriarchal world. Here, the *vara* becomes a feminist lens, illuminating Draupadī's resilience and Kuntī's quiet strength.

Curses, too, find nuanced retellings. Ahalyā's *śāpa*, traditionally a tale of punishment, is reimagined in modern works like Koral Dasgupta's *Ahalyā* as a narrative of introspection and liberation; her petrified state a metaphor for societal oppression, her redemption a reclaiming of voice. These literary adaptations transform curses and boons from divine mandates into human stories, exploring themes of choice, consequence, and redemption that resonate with modern readers.

Cinema: Visual Spectacles of Cosmic Justice

Indian cinema, with its kaleidoscopic lens, amplifies the drama of curses and boons, rendering them as visual spectacles that captivate the heart. Films like *Bāhubali* (2015) weave *śāpa* and *vara* into epic narratives, where a curse upon a kingdom mirrors the Purāṇic motif of collective retribution, and a hero's boon-like strength restores *dharma*. In *Devdas* (2002), a modern retelling of Sarat Chandra Chattopadhyay's novel, the curse-like suffering of Paro, bound by societal norms, echoes Ahalyā's silent endurance, while Devdas's self-inflicted ruin mirrors the consequences of misused boons. Regional cinema, too, embraces these motifs: Tamil films like *Kandhan Karunai* (1967) depict Murugan's boon to Idumban, transforming his curse into a sacred duty, a visual hymn to redemption.

Bollywood and regional filmmakers use curses and boons to explore universal themes love, betrayal, and justice while grounding them in Indian ethos. The *śāpa* becomes a cinematic device for conflict, driving narratives toward resolution, while the *vara* symbolizes hope, often visualized through divine interventions or heroic triumphs, making these motifs accessible to diverse audiences.

Theatre: Intimate Reflections of Divine Will

In the intimate space of Indian theatre, curses and boons are reimagined as dialogues between the human and divine, their immediacy amplified by live performance. Plays like Girish Karnad's *Nagamandala* project folk motifs of *śāpa* and *vara* into tales of human desire, where a woman's curse upon her unfaithful husband mirrors Gāndhārī's wrath, yet her eventual boon-like forgiveness reflects the redemptive power of love. Contemporary theatre groups, such as Chennai's Perch Collective, adapt stories like the *Samudra Manthana*, portraying Durvāsas' curse and Viṣṇu's boon as allegories for societal imbalance and restoration, their minimalist stages evoking the cosmic scale through human emotion.

Theatre's intimacy allows for nuanced explorations of gender and power, with women like Kaikeyī or the *Ṛṣikanyās* reimagined as complex figures navigating divine and patriarchal constraints. These performances transform curses and boons into mirrors of the human psyche, inviting audiences to reflect on morality and agency in a modern context.

Persistence of These Concepts in Contemporary Culture

The motifs of curses and boons endure in contemporary Indian culture, their resonance undimmed by the passage of centuries. In urban India, where skyscrapers rise alongside ancient temples, these concepts permeate popular consciousness through festivals, rituals, and storytelling. The festival of Thaipusam in Tamilnadu re-enacts Murugan's boon to Idumban, with devotees carrying kāvadi as a symbol of penance and divine favour, a living testament to the vara's power. In Bengal, Mā Manasā's worship, tied to her curses and boons, thrives in rural rituals, her stories retold in village fairs, blending myth with modernity.

In popular culture, curses and boons are manifested as metaphors for fate and fortune. Bollywood dialogues often invoke the "curse of a wronged woman" or the "boon of divine blessings," embedding these motifs in everyday language. Social media platforms, like X, buzz with references to mythological *śāpa* and *vara*, with users drawing parallels between ancient curses and modern struggles, such as societal pressures or personal betrayals. These concepts, rooted in *ṛta*, resonate as timeless archetypes, offering frameworks to navigate the complexities of contemporary life be it the curse-like weight of societal expectations or the boon-like hope of personal triumph.

Indian Television Mythological Serials and Their Influence

Indian television, with its vast reach, has been a powerful medium for reimagining curses and boons, particularly through mythological serials that bring Purāṇic tales to millions. Shows like *Devon Ke Dev... Mahādev* (2011–2014) and *Mahābhārata* (2013–2014) dramatize these motifs with cinematic grandeur, making them accessible to urban and rural audiences alike. In *Devon Ke Dev... Mahadev*, the *Samudra Manthana* is a visual spectacle, with Durvāsas' curse upon the *devas* and Viṣṇu's boon of *amṛta* portrayed as pivotal moments of cosmic balance. The serial humanizes Śiva's compassion as he consumes *hālāhala*, emphasizing the boon of divine sacrifice, resonating with viewers' aspirations for selflessness.

Mahābhārata reimagines Gāndhārī's curse upon Kṛṣṇa as a mother's anguished cry, her *śāpa* a climactic moment that underscores the consequences of war, while Kuntī's boon shapes the Pāṇḍavas' destinies, portrayed as a woman's triumph over adversity. Serials like *Siya Ke Ram* (2015–2016) reframe Ahalyā's curse as a feminist narrative, her petrified state a symbol of silenced women, her redemption a celebration of agency, inspiring viewers to question patriarchal norms.

These serials wield immense influence, shaping cultural perceptions by blending myth with modern values. Their serialized format allows for deep exploration of *śāpa* and *vara*, with episodes delving into characters' motivations Kaikeyī's ambition, Gāndhārī's grief, or Ahalyā's resilience. Broadcast into homes across India, these shows make mythology a living tradition, their exaggerated emotions and lavish visuals amplifying the drama of curses and boons. They inspire devotion, spark debates on X about *dharma* and gender, and reinforce the moral lessons of *ṛta*, ensuring that these ancient motifs remain vibrant in the collective imagination.

Conclusion

In modern India, curses and boons are taken as enduring motifs, their essence rekindled through literature, cinema, theatre, and television. From the introspective pages of novels to the grandiose spectacles of films, from the intimate dialogues of plays to the serialized dramas of mythological serials, *śāpa* and *vara* are reimagined as mirrors of the human soul. They persist in contemporary culture, compromising ancient wisdom into festivals, rituals, and digital conversations, offering solace and insight in a rapidly changing world. Indian television, with its unparalleled reach, breathes life into these motifs, making Purāṇic tales a shared heritage that bridges generations. In their luminous interplay, curses and boons remind us that the eternal rhythm of *ṛta* with its cycles of trial and triumph, retribution and redemption continues to guide the heart toward *dharma*, illuminating the path to the divine in the modern age.

❑

Conclusion

Thus, in the multiple dimensions of Indian mythology, where the divine and mortal assemble in an eternal dance of *ṛta*, the spoken word embodied in curses (*śāpa*) and boons (*vara*) spins the threads of cosmic consequence that shimmer across ages. These sacred utterances, whether whispered by sages in forest hermitages or thundered by gods in celestial courts, are not mere words but potent forces that forsee destinies, balance *dharma*, and illuminate the human soul. From the cosmic churn of the *Samudra Manthana* to the intimate struggles of village folklore, from the anguished curses of Gāndhārī to the redemptive boons of Kuntī, *śāpa* and *vara* pulse with the rhythm of existence, their power undimmed in modern retellings. This concluding chapter reflects on the enduring legacy of these divine decrees, their philosophical relevance in today's world, and their role as moral and metaphysical commentary, offering a bridge between ancient wisdom and contemporary seeking.

Recapitulation of Findings

Throughout the chapters of this exploration, we have traversed the manifold landscapes of Indian mythology, uncovering the multifaceted roles of curses and boons. In the *Purāṇas*, they orchestrate cosmological events, as seen in the *Samudra Manthana*, where Durvāsas' *śāpa* sparked a divine quest and Viṣṇu's *vara* restored cosmic balance. They transform gods, demons, and mortals, as with Jaya and Vijaya, whose curse-driven incarnations led to liberation, or the Pāṇḍavas, born of Kuntī's boon to uphold *dharma*. In regional tales, from Odisha's Ākhaṇḍalamaṇi to Bengal's Mā Manasā, *śāpa* and *vara* bind communities to their deities, weaving lessons of humility and devotion into village life. Gender dynamics reveal women like Kaikeyī and Ahalyā as both agents and victims, their stories challenging patriarchal constraints while affirming feminine resilience. Modern retellings in literature, cinema, and television breathe new life into these motifs, making them mirrors of contemporary struggles and aspirations.

Curses and boons emerge as dual forces retribution and redemption, disruption and restoration interwoven with the doctrine of karma. They are not arbitrary but purposeful, governed by conditions that reflect *ṛta*, ensuring that every act ripples through the cosmos. Their psychological archetypes reward, punishment, desire, and fear resonate with universal human experiences, while their moral lessons guide behaviour toward righteousness. In every narrative, from the epic to the folk, the spoken word reigns supreme, its power to shape destinies a testament to the sanctity of intention and utterance in Indian thought.

The Philosophical Relevance of *Śāpa* and *Vara* Today

In an era of rapid change, where technology and globalization reshape human connections, the philosophical relevance of *śāpa* and *vara* endures as a beacon of timeless wisdom. These motifs, rooted in the sanctity of the spoken word, remind us of the power of intention in a world where words spoken, written, or tweeted carry unprecedented reach. A curse, as a symbol of consequence, mirrors the modern struggle with accountability, where hasty words or actions can ripple through social media, shaping reputations and relationships. The *śāpa* of Gāndhārī, born of grief, finds echoes in contemporary calls for justice, where voices raised against oppression carry the weight of moral outrage, demanding redress.

Boons, as emblems of aspiration, resonate in today's pursuit of empowerment and opportunity. Kuntī's *vara*, birthing heroes through divine grace, parallels the modern quest for agency, be it through education, innovation, or activism. Yet, like Rāvaṇa's boon, which led to hubris, modern gifts wealth, influence, technology carries the risk of misuse, urging restraint and responsibility. The interplay of *śāpa* and *vara* with *karma* offers a philosophical lens for navigating ethical dilemmas, reminding us that every choice, whether a tweet or a promise, weaves our destiny within the cosmic order.

Philosophically, these motifs affirm the interconnectedness of all beings, a principle vital in an age of environmental and social crises. The Purāṇic vision of *ṛta* where curses and boons balance *dharma* invites reflection on our collective responsibility to restore harmony, whether through sustainable practices or compassionate dialogue. In a world, where words can wound or heal the enduring relevance of *śāpa* and *vara* lies in their call to wield speech with intention, aligning our voices with the eternal rhythm of truth.

Myth as Moral and Metaphysical Commentary

Indian mythology, through the lens of curses and boons, serves as a profound moral and metaphysical commentary, offering insights into the nature of existence and the human condition. Morally, *śāpa* and *vara* are compasses for navigating *dharma*, teaching humility, resilience, and accountability. The curse of Ahalyā, though punitive, becomes a journey of redemption, urging us to see suffering as a crucible for growth. The boon of Arjuna's Pāśupata weapon, granted through penance, underscores the virtue of discipline, a reminder that true power is earned through sacrifice.

Metaphysically, these motifs illuminate the interplay of free will and destiny within *ṛta*. Jaya and Vijaya's curse, tempered by the choice of adversarial lives, reveals that even divine decrees are woven into the karmic fabric, where choice shapes liberation. The *Samudra Manthana*, sparked by a curse and resolved by a boon, mirrors the cosmic cycle of chaos and creation, suggesting that existence itself is a dance of opposites, harmonized by divine intent. These myths, far from being mere stories, are philosophical treatises, inviting us to ponder the nature of power, the weight of words, and the eternal quest for *mokṣa*.

In modern contexts, these narratives resonate as allegories for personal and societal transformation. The curse-like weight of systemic inequities or the boon-like promise of collective action reflect the Purāṇic vision of balance, urging us to align with *dharma* in our choices. As moral and metaphysical commentary, *śāpa* and *vara* transcend time, their spoken words echoing as calls to live with intention, compassion, and reverence for the cosmic order.

The spoken word, as *śāpa* and *vara*, remains the beating heart of Indian mythology, its power to shape destinies as potent today as in the age of sages and gods. These divine decrees, weaving through Purāṇic epics, regional folklore, and modern retellings, are more than narrative devices; they are mirrors of the soul, reflecting the interplay of *karma* and *ṛta*. Their philosophical relevance endures, guiding us to wield words with intention, to seek balance in a fractured world, and to embrace the redemptive potential of suffering and grace. As moral and metaphysical commentary, *śāpa* and *vara* transcend time, their echoes in literature, cinema, and ritual a testament to the eternal wisdom of Indian mythology. In their in there multiple working of themes, we find not only the stories of gods and mortals but the timeless truth of our own existence, forever bound to the sacred power of the spoken word.

❑

Appendix

Curses and Boons in Indian Mythology

In the vast horizon of Indian mythology, curses (*śāpa*) and boons (*vara*) project life's destiny, by intervening the lives of gods, mortals, and celestial beings. These divine pronouncements, bestowed by sages, deities, or cosmic forces, carry profound consequences, often altering the course of existence across lifetimes. Below is a comprehensive catalogue of notable curses and boons, drawn from the epics *Rāmāyaṇa* and *Mahābhārata*, as well as other Purāṇic narratives. Each entry is imbued with the grandeur and mystique befitting the timeless tales of Bhārata.

Curses

Tārā's Curse on Śrī Rāma

Tārā, the grieving wife of Vālī, cursed Śrī Rāma after he slew her husband during Vālī's duel with Sugrīva. In her anguish, she declared that Rāma would lose Sītā soon after regaining her and that Sītā would return to the earth. Furthermore, Tārā foretold that in Rāma's next birth as Śrī Kṛṣṇa, he would be killed by Vālī, reborn as a hunter. This curse found fulfillment in the *Rāmāyaṇa* and later in the *Bhāgavata Purāṇa*.

Sanatkumāras' Curse on Jaya and Vijaya

The gatekeepers of Vaikuṇṭha, Jaya and Vijaya, were cursed by the Sanatkumāras for barring their entry to Lord Viṣṇu's abode. The curse condemned them to mortal births as *asuras*: Hiraṇyakaśipu and Hiraṇyākṣa in the *Satya Yuga*, Rāvaṇa and Kumbhakarṇa in the *Tretā Yuga*, and Śiśupāla and Dantavakra in the *Dvāpara Yuga*. Viṣṇu took four *avatāras* Varāha, Narasiṃha, Rāma, and Kṛṣṇa to liberate them.

Śravaṇa Kumāra's Parents' Curse on Daśaratha

The aged parents of Śravaṇa Kumāra, mistakenly killed by King Daśaratha, cursed him to suffer the agony of separation from his son. This prophecy manifested when Rāma was exiled due to Kaikeyī's boons, leading to Daśaratha's untimely death.

Sage Gautama's Curse on Ahalyā

Discovering Ahalyā's infidelity with Indra, Sage Gautama cursed her to become a stone until liberated by Śrī Rāma's touch. This tale, narrated in the *Bālakāṇḍa* of the *Rāmāyaṇa*, underscores the redemptive power of divine grace.

Sage Gautama's Curse on Indra

For his transgression with Ahalyā, Gautama cursed Indra to bear a thousand female genitals (*sahasrayoni*). Later, this curse was transformed into a boon, granting Indra a thousand eyes, earning him the epithet *Sahasrākṣa* (Thousand-Eyed).

Sages' Curse on Hanumān

In his mischievous childhood, Hanumān vexed several

sages, who cursed him to forget his divine powers until reminded by another. In the Kiṣkindhā Kāṇḍa and *Sundarā Kāṇḍa* of the *Rāmāyaṇa*, Jambavanta's words rekindle Hanumān's strength, enabling him to undertake his heroic quest for Sītā.

Sage's Curse on Añjanā

Añjanā, an apsarā, was cursed by a meditating *vānara* sage to become a *vānara* herself upon falling in love. Her act of throwing fruits at the sage provoked this *śāpa*, which was later absolved through Brahmā's *vara*, fulfilled by her giving birth to Hanumān, an incarnation of Śiva.

Nārada's Curse on Viṣṇu

Sage Nārada, enraged by a divine illusion, cursed Viṣṇu to rely on a *vānara* in his mortal form. This manifested in the *Rāmāyaṇa*, where Hanumān's unwavering devotion aided Śrī Rāma's mission.

Gāndhārī's Curse on Śrī Kṛṣṇa

Holding Kṛṣṇa responsible for the *Mahābhārata* war, Gāndhārī cursed him to meet an ordinary end and his Yādava clan to perish in infighting. Thirty-six years later, her words came to pass, as detailed in the *Bhāgavata Purāṇa*.

Sages' Curse on Sāmba

Sāmba, Kṛṣṇa's son, and his companions mocked sages Viśvāmitra, Durvāsā, Vasiṣṭha, and Nārada. The sages cursed Sāmba to give birth to an iron lump that would destroy the Yādava race, a prophecy fulfilled in the *Mahābhārata's* aftermath.

Śrī Kṛṣṇa's Curse on Sāmba

Kṛṣṇa cursed his son Sāmba with leprosy for his indiscretions, a divine reprimand to curb his arrogance.

Śrī Kṛṣṇa's Curse on Aśvatthāmā

After Aśvatthāmā attempted to kill the unborn Parīkṣit with the Brahmāstra, Kṛṣṇa cursed him to wander immortal, afflicted with suffering, as recounted in the *Mahābhārata*.

Ūrvaśī's Curse on Arjuna

When Arjuna spurned Ūrvaśī's advances, she cursed him to become a eunuch. Later, she mitigated the curse to last only a year, which Arjuna utilized during his ajñātavāsa in the *Mahābhārata*.

Yudhiṣṭhira's Curse on Womankind

Learning from Kuntī that Karṇa was his elder brother, Yudhiṣṭhira cursed all women to be unable to conceal secrets, a reaction to Kuntī's hidden truth about Karṇa's birth, influenced by Durvāsā's boon.

Paraśurāma's Curse on Karṇa

Discovering Karṇa's kṣatriya lineage, Paraśurāma cursed him to forget the Brahmāstra *mantra* at a critical moment, a *śāpa* that proved fatal in the *Mahābhārata's* Kurukṣetra war.

Bhūmi Devī's Curse on Karṇa

For causing her distress, *Bhūmi* Devī cursed Karṇa that his chariot wheel would sink into the earth during battle, sealing his doom in the *Mahābhārata*.

Brāhmaṇa's Curse on Karṇa

After Karṇa accidentally killed a brāhmaṇa's cow, the brāhmaṇa cursed him to die helplessly, mirroring the cow's fate, a prophecy fulfilled during his final battle.

Vasiṣṭha's Curse on the Vasus

The Vasus, for stealing Vasiṣṭha's divine cow Nandini, were cursed to be born as mortals. This led to the birth of Bhīṣma, as narrated in the *Mahābhārata*.

Rishi Kindama's Curse on Pāṇḍu

Pāṇḍu, mistakenly killing Sage Kindama and his wife during their union, was cursed to die if he ever embraced a woman. This led to his death with Madrī, as detailed in the *Mahābhārata*.

Śukrācārya's Curse on Yayāti

For secretly wedding Śarmiṣṭhā, Śukrācārya cursed King Yayāti with premature old age. Yayāti was allowed to exchange his state with a willing person, and his son Puru accepted, becoming his successor.

Śiva's Curse on Brahmā

For lying about reaching the end of Śiva's liṅga, Śiva cursed Brahmā to be denied worship. The ketakī flower, complicit in the lie, was also barred from worship.

Sarasvatī's Curse on Brahmā

Irritated by Brahmā's undue advances, Sarasvatī cursed him to remain unworshipped, reinforcing Śiva's decree.

Brahmā's Curse on Śiva

When Śiva severed Brahmā's fifth head (mistaken by Pārvatī for Śiva), Brahmā cursed Śiva to bear the head, causing insatiable hunger. Pārvatī, with Viṣṇu's aid, freed Śiva from this burden.

Gaṇeśa's Curse on Candra (Moon)

Gaṇeśa cursed the moon for mocking him, decreeing that none would gaze upon it on *Gaṇeśa Caturthī* without facing misfortune.

Nārada's Curse on Kubera's Sons

Nalakūvara and Maṇigrīva, Kubera's sons, were cursed by Nārada to become twin trees for their insolence while bathing naked. Śrī Kṛṣṇa later liberated them, as described in the *Bhāgavata Purāṇa.*

Vasiṣṭha's Curse on Satyavrata (Triśaṅku)

For stealing and consuming Vasiṣṭha's cow, Satyavrata was cursed with a debilitating disease. Viśvāmitra later attempted to send him to heaven in his mortal form.

Rādhā and Śrīdāma's Mutual Curses

Rādhā cursed Śrīdāma to be born in a low family, and he retaliated, cursing her to be separated from Kṛṣṇa for a hundred years, a tale from the *Bhāgavata Purāṇa.*

Brahmā's Curse on Śantanu and Gaṅgā

For their celestial indiscretions, Brahmā cursed Śantanu (*Mahābhiṣaka*) and Gaṅgā to be born as mortals, leading to their earthly lives in the *Mahābhārata.*

Sarasvatī's Curse on Lakṣmī

Sarasvatī cursed Lakṣmī to be born as a tree. In retaliation, Gaṅgā cursed Sarasvatī to become Brahmā's wife, while Sarasvatī cursed Gaṅgā to become a holy river, absolving sins.

Kabandha's Curse

The rākṣasa Kabandha, cursed to remain a monstrous form, was freed by Śrī Rāma's slaying. He advised Rāma to ally with Sugrīva, aiding the quest for Sītā in the *Rāmāyaṇa.*

Boons

Brahmā's Boon to Meghanāda

Brahmā granted Meghanāda invincibility in battle unless his *yajña* to Nikumbalā was disrupted. Lakṣmaṇa destroyed the *yajña*, leading to Meghanāda's defeat in the *Rāmāyaṇa.*

Vṛddhakṣatra's Boon to Jayadratha

Jayadratha's father, Vṛddhakṣatra, blessed him that anyone causing his head to fall on the ground would die with their head bursting. Arjuna ensured Jayadratha's head fell into his father's lap, fulfilling the boon fatally.

Śiva's Boon to Jayadratha

Śiva granted Jayadratha the ability to hold all Pāṇḍavas except Arjuna for a day in battle, contributing to Abhimanyu's death in the *Mahābhārata.*

Śantanu's Boon to Bhīṣma

Śantanu blessed his son Devavrata (Bhīṣma) to choose his time of death, following Bhīṣma's vow of celibacy, as narrated in the *Mahābhārata.*

Gāndhārī's Boon to Duryodhana

Gāndhārī bestowed upon Duryodhana a boon of near-invincibility, making his body as strong as a diamond, except for his thighs, which proved his vulnerability in the *Mahābhārata*.

Durvāsā's Boon to Kuntī

Pleased with Kuntī's service, Durvāsā granted her a mantra to summon any god to beget a son. This led to the birth of the Pāṇḍavas, as detailed in the *Mahābhārata*.

Paraśara's Boon to Satyavatī

Sage Paraśara blessed Satyavatī with a divine fragrance, transforming her life, as recounted in the *Mahābhārata*.

Vālī's Boon

Vālī was blessed that half his opponent's strength would transfer to him in combat, necessitating Rāma's covert attack in the *Rāmāyaṇa*.

Paraśurāma's Boon to Karṇa

Despite cursing him, Paraśurāma blessed Karṇa with everlasting fame, ensuring his legacy endures in the *Mahābhārata*.

Brahmā's Boon to Hiraṇyākṣa

Hiraṇyākṣa received a boon from Brahmā that no god, demon, beast, or human could kill him. Viṣṇu's Varāha *avatāra* circumvented this, slaying him in the *Bhāgavata Purāṇa*.

Brahmā's Boon to Hiraṇyakaśipu

Hiraṇyakaśipu's boon ensured he could not be killed

by day or night, inside or outside, by human or beast. Viṣṇu's Narasiṃha *avatāra* defeated him, fulfilling Prahlāda's devotion in the *Bhāgavata Purāṇa*.

Śrī Kṛṣṇa's Boon to Śrutiśrava

Kṛṣṇa promised his aunt Śrutiśrava to forgive Śiśupāla's hundred misdeeds before slaying him, a vow kept in the *Mahābhārata*.

Śiva's Boon to Arjuna

Śiva granted Arjuna the Pāśupatāstra, a formidable weapon, aiding him in the *Mahābhārata's* Kurukṣetra war.

Śiva's Boon to Gaṇeśa

Śiva decreed that Gaṇeśa be worshipped before all undertakings, cementing his primacy in rituals across Hindu traditions.

Boon to Madhu and Kaiṭabha

These demons were blessed to die only at their own will, yet Viṣṇu outwitted them, as narrated in the *Bhāgavata Purāṇa*.

Brahmā's Boon to Añjanā

Brahmā absolved Añjanā's curse, declaring her liberation upon giving birth to Hanumān, Śiva's incarnation, as per the *Rāmāyaṇa*.

Boons to Hanumān

Brahmā's Boon: No weapon could harm Hanumān, allowing him to honour the Brahmāstra by submitting to capture in the *Rāmāyaṇa*.

Sūrya's Boon: Hanumān gained *laghimā* (smallness)

and *garimā* (greatness), enabling him to bypass Sursa in the *Sundara Kāṇḍa*.

Karṇa's Boon to Kuntī

Karṇa promised Kuntī to spare four Pāṇḍavas and not reuse a weapon against Arjuna, ensuring her five sons' survival, as seen in the *Mahābhārata*.

Daśaratha's Boons to Kaikeyī

During a battle, Kaikeyī saved Daśaratha, earning two boons. She later used them to exile Rāma and crown Bharata, pivotal to the *Rāmāyaṇa*.

Śiva's Boon to Draupadī (Desired Husbands)

Draupadī sought a husband with fourteen qualities, and Śiva granted her five husbands the Pāṇḍavas fulfilling her wish in the *Mahābhārata*.

Śiva's Boon to Draupadī (Virginity)

Śiva blessed Draupadī to regain her virginity each morning after bathing, enabling her to be the wife of all five Pāṇḍavas simultaneously.

This appendix encapsulates the profound interplay of *śāpa* and *vara*, where divine justice and mercy converge to shape the cosmic narrative of Indian mythology. These tales, resonating with moral and spiritual depth, continue to inspire awe and reverence.

Glossary of Sanskrit Terms

***Adharma*:** The shadow cast by the neglect of righteousness; the antithesis of *dharma*, representing actions that disrupt the cosmic harmony of *ṛta*.

Ātma-vala: The radiant strength of the soul, forged through spiritual discipline and *tapas*.

Bhakti: The luminous path of devotion, a heartfelt surrender to the divine that often elicits *varas*.

***Dharma*:** The eternal law of righteousness, the golden thread that binds individual actions to the cosmic order of *ṛta*.

Divya-śakti: The celestial power wielded by gods and sages, the force behind the pronouncement of *śāpa* and *vara*.

Karma: The inexorable law of cause and effect, weaving every action into the tapestry of destiny.

Karuṇā : The tender compassion that softens the heart of the divine, often leading to boons or the mitigation of curses.

Krodha : The fiery wrath of the righteous, the spark that ignites a *śāpa*.

Mokṣa: The sublime liberation from the cycle of *saṃsāra*, the ultimate *vara* sought by devotees.

Pātratā: The worthiness of a soul, forged in *tapas* and sincerity, that qualifies one for divine boons.

Ṛta: The cosmic order, the principle of truth and harmony that governs the universe.

Sādhanā: The disciplined spiritual practice that aligns the soul with divine will, often a prerequisite for boons.

Saṃsāra: The cyclical realm of birth and death, where curses and boons shape the soul's journey.

Samudra Manthana: The churning of the cosmic ocean, a Purāṇic event yielding divine treasures.

Śāpa: A curse, a potent pronouncement of misfortune uttered by sages or deities, often as a corrective to *adharma*.

Tapas: Austerity or penance, spiritual discipline that grants power to sages and devotees.

Vāk: The sacred power of the spoken word, capable of creating or destroying destinies.

Vara: A boon, a divine gift or blessing granting power, prosperity, or liberation, often with conditions.

Yajña: The sacred ritual sacrifice, a conduit for invoking divine boons and averting curses.

❑

Bibliography

Acharya, Tarkaratna Panchanan (ed.); *Agni Purāṇa*, Naba Bharata Publisher, Kolkata-09, 2015.

Acharya, Tarkaratna Panchanan (ed.); *Bhavisya Purāṇa*, Naba Bharata Publisher, Kolkata-09, 2015.

Acharya, Tarkaratna Panchanan (ed.); *Brahmānda Purāṇa*, Naba Bharata Publisher, Kolkata-09, 2015.

Acharya, Tarkaratna Panchanan (ed.); *Garuda Purāṇa*, Naba Bharata Publisher, Kolkata-09, 2015.

Acharya, Tarkaratna Panchanan (ed.); *Kurma Purāṇa*, Naba Bharata Publisher, Kolkata-09, 2015.

Acharya, Tarkaratna Panchanan (ed.); *Liṅga Purāṇa*, Naba Bharata Publisher, Kolkata-09, 2015.

Acharya, Tarkaratna Panchanan (ed.); *Mahābhāgavata Purāṇa*, Naba Bharata Publisher, Kolkata-09, 2015.

Acharya, Tarkaratna Panchanan (ed.); *Pama Purāṇa*, Naba Bharata Publisher, Kolkata-09, 2015.

Acharya, Tarkaratna Panchanan (ed.); Skanda Purāṇa, Naba Bharata Publisher, Kolkata-09, 2015.

Acharya, Tarkaratna Panchanan (ed.); *Varāha Purāṇa*, naba Bharat Publisher, Kolkta-09, 2015.

Acharya, Tarkaratna Panchanan (ed.); *Visṇu Purāṇa*, naba Bharata Publisher, Kolkata-09, 2015.

Acharya, Tarkaratna Panchanan (ed.); *Brahma Purāṇa*,

Naba Bharata Publisher, Kolkata-09, 2015.

Acharya, Tarkaratna Panchanan (ed.); *Matsya Purāṇa*, Naba Bharata Publisher, Kolkata-09, 2015.

Acharya, Tarkaratna Panchanan (ed.); *Vāmana Purāṇa*, Naba Bharata Publisher, Kolkata - 09, 2015.

Agarwal, V.S.; "*Matsya Purāṇa: A Study*; All India Kashiraj Trust, Ramnagar Fort, Varanasi, 1963.

Basudevānanda, Swami, *Srimadbhagavadgitā with Śamkarabhāṣya*, Udvodhan Karyalaya, Kolkata. 1986.

Benarjee, Jayantānuja, *Samājvijñaner drṣṭite Bhagavadgita*, Allied Publishers Limited, Kolkata. 1994.

Buhler, G., The Laws of Manu. In Sacred Books of the East, Vol. 25, Clarendon Press, 1886.

Gambhirananda, Swāmī, *Srimadbhagavadgitā with Śamkara Bhāṣya*, Udvodhan Karyalaya, Kolkata .1986.

Gandhi, M.K, *The Bhagavadgita*, Orient Paper Backs, Delhi.1980.

Goldman, Robert P., and Sally J. Sutherland Goldman. *The Rāmāyaṇa of Vālmīki: An Epic of Ancient India*, Volume I: Bālakāṇḍa. Princeton University Press, 1984.

Krishnamachariar, M., *History of Classical Sanskrit Literature*, Motilal Banarasi Dass, Delhi, 1970.

Kumari, Sujata, *Indian Culture in Mahabharata*, Neha Pustak Kendra, Delhi, 2016.

Lalye, P.G., *Curses and Boons in the Valmiki Ramayana*, Bharatiya Kala Prakashan, Delhi, 2008.

Lutgendorf, Philip, *The Life of a Text: Performing the Rāmcaritmānas of Tulsidas*, University of California Press, 1991.

Patil, D.R.; *Cultural History from the Vāyu Purāṇa*, Deccan College, Poona, 1946.

Pollock, Sheldon, *The Rāmāyaṇa of Vālmīki: An Epic*

of Ancient India, Volume III: Araṇyakāṇḍa. Princeton University Press, 1991.

Pusalkar, A.D., *Studies in the Epics and Purāṇas of India*, Bharatiya Vidya Bhavan, Mumbai, 1967

Rgveda (with Sāyana's Commentary in 5 Volumes), Vaidika Samshodhan Mandal, Poona, 1933, 1936, 1941, 1946, 1951.

Śāstri, Vāsudeva Lakṣmaṇa, *Rāmāyaṇam, (With Tilaka Ṭīkā)*, Nirṇaya Sāgar Press, Mumbai, 1930.

Shastri, Satya Vrata, *The Rāmāyaṇa – Linguistic Study*, Munshi Ram Manohar Lal Oriental Publishers and Booksellers, Delhi,

Singh, Anand. S.; *Historical and Cultural Roots of the Purāṇas (Proceeding)*, Iswar Saran Degree College, University of Allahabad, U.P. 2011.

Singh, Bhagavat Prasad, *Rāmāyaṇam*, Chowkhamba Sanskrit Series Office, Varanasi, 1973.

Singh, M.R.; *Geographical Data In The Early Purāṇas – A Critical Study*, Punthi Pustak Publisher, Kolkata-4, 1972.

Sircar, Dinesh Chandra, *Studies in the Yuga Purāṇa and other texts*, Oriental Publishers, Delhi, 1974.

Srinivasachariar, Pandit A.M., *The Mahabharata*, Kuppuswami Sastri Research Institute, Chennai, 2015.

Upadhaya, Baladeva; *Purāṇa Vimarsa*, Chaukamba Vidyabhavana, Varanasi, 2010.

Vyāsa, Ramakṛṣṇa Ṭi, *Vālmīki Rāmāyaṇam*, Oriental Institute, Baroda, 1992.

Woods, Julian F., *The Phenomenon of Boon and Curse in the Mahabharata (with Special Reference to the Adiparva)*, McGill University, Montreal, 1983.

❑

Black Eagle Books

www.blackeaglebooks.org
info@blackeaglebooks.org

Black Eagle Books, an independent publisher, was founded as a nonprofit organization in April, 2019. It is our mission to connect and engage the Indian diaspora and the world at large with the best of works of world literature published on a collaborative platform, with special emphasis on foregrounding Contemporary Classics and New Writing.

www.ingramcontent.com/pod-product-compliance
Lightning Source LLC
Chambersburg PA
CBHW050416110726
47899CB00008B/2733

* 9 7 8 1 6 4 5 6 0 7 4 1 0 *